A CERTAIN
SYMPATHY OF
SCRIPTURES

A CERTAIN
SYMPATHY OF
SCRIPTURES

BIBLICAL AND QURANIC

KENNETH CRAGG

sussex
ACADEMIC
PRESS

BRIGHTON • *PORTLAND*

2 4 6 8 10 9 7 5 3

First published 2004, reprinted 2005 in Great Britain by
SUSSEX ACADEMIC PRESS
PO Box 2950
Brighton BN2 5SP

and in the United States of America by
SUSSEX ACADEMIC PRESS
920 NE 58th Ave   Suite 300
Portland, Oregon 97213-3786

British Library Cataloguing in Publication Data
A CIP catalogue record for this book is available from the British Library.

Library of Congress Cataloging-in-Publication Data
Cragg, Kenneth.
     A certain sympathy of scriptures : biblical and
quranic / Kenneth Cragg.
     p. cm.
     Includes bibliographical references and index.
     ISBN 1-84519-012-2 (alk. paper)
     1. Bible—Criticism, Textual. 2. Koran—
Criticism, Textual. 3. Islam—Relations—
Christianity. 4. Christianity and other religions—
Islam. 5. Koran—Relation to the Bible. I. Title.
BS471.C73 2004
220.6—dc22
                                                    2004000504
                                                         CIP

The Author and Publisher acknowledge with thanks the financial assistance of
the Altajir World of Islam Trust.

Typeset and designed by G&G Editorial, Brighton
Printed by TJ International, Padstow, Cornwall
This book is printed on acid-free paper.

Contents

———

Preface and Precaution
Bible and Qur'an in Inter-Study

—

I

'I had a lover's quarrel with the world' was how Robert Frost, the wistful twentieth-century American poet, reflected on his life and writing. It was, by his philosophy, the very love which necessitated the quarrel. For only out of his passionate intensity, which 'had miles to go before I sleep', did he duly read the burdened scene through which he passed.[1] The paradox he registered belongs squarely with the business of religion also. How do we reconcile the themes of wonder, gratitude and moral duty with the experiences of anxiety and tragedy which seem to contradict them? Why should the impulses to faith be at times so far at odds with the actualities as they seem around us everyday? Yet with these there would be no 'quarrel' were there no 'love' to prompt it in our heart or vex it in the mind.

Any intelligent 'lover's quarrel with the world' is at once busy with the lovers' quarrels of religion. The great faiths of history are certainly communities of 'passionate attachment',[2] bonded by long-lasting tradition and by strong affinities that are ethnic, linguistic, territorial and national. They have rites and liturgies congenial only to themselves and, therefore, are in large measure secessionist in respect of humanity at large or, if not separatist in intention (given their will to 'mission'), prove so the more in fact by that very will. For these marks of identity are at home in structures of doctrine and systems of law or custom which more readily exclusify than embrace – all of which tends towards a 'non-lovers' quarrel' of religions. It is one of which there have been ample evidences along all the centuries.

Those evidences have been notably acute in 'the aliens' quarrel' between Islam and Christianity – or perhaps we should more hopefully say, between Muslims and Christians. The long scenario is well enough known and frequently rehearsed. For the history – its telling, sifting and discerning – are part of the equation.

The aim of the present study is to see (not 'invent') the grounds on which it might become in fact 'a lovers' quarrel' insofar as 'quarrel' or 'inter-question' it must always remain. The intention is to identify how and where, in loyalty to their respective Scriptures, the Qur'an and the Bible, those who have so long proved 'aliens' to each other, might instead recognize the partial perceptions of Allah, of God, they authentically share and more avowedly proceed upon them. There will still be a mitigated 'quarrel' with which they may the better live.

'Recognize' and 'proceed upon' are crucial here. For it has been said in this context that the parties have managed to co-exist amicably in many places and at many times and that this might well be resumed if only busy 'theologians' did not persist in troubling it with faith-formula better left to intelligent neglect. That *de facto* situation of viable co-existence, thankful as it was, was all too often had at the price of acute psychic or political inferiorization, *dhimmi* status, social privation, and forfeiture of spiritual freedom of conscience and allegiance. These were a price of compatibility no longer fit for the contemporary world and inhibiting the honesty in which alone any and every religion must consciously under-take the issues of a now global scene, and do so in articulate mutual reckoning with what each holds for truth and tells in witness.[3] Current history is no place for conspiracies of silence in which we privately believe our own, staying glaringly incommunicado.

II

It is this readiness to belong intelligently with each other because of where we must both belong in current time that suggests the assonance of the book's title. 'Scriptures' are the realm for both parties where open mutu-ality must start and continue, since these are the ultimate court of appeal – taxing as recourse is – for authority and meaning. 'A certain sympathy' on the part of readership exchanged is aptly so described. The word 'certain' in such a context has the right measure as in the Arabic *fulan*, or the Gospels' usage: 'A certain man had two sons . . .', i.e. anyone at all, the less specific the more inclusive, a sort of non-identity the more real by being more approximate. 'Sympathy', too, is neither 'antipathy', nor 'indifference'. It wants to participate, being neither intimate nor remote. Such, at least at the outset, is what we most need. For the proposal that the 'quarrels' Muslims have long had with the Bible, and Christians with the Qur'an could ever be those of 'lovers' will seem a far-fetched idea. If, as honestly must remain the case, 'quarrel' has to be the word, can it ever be 'in lover's part' either way? Will it not still be, as too far hitherto, an 'aliens' quarrel'? For the dissuasives are many and deep-seated in both traditions. The will to violent alienation spells doom.

It becomes necessary to ask whether, in fact, the issues were as alien-ating as the enmity took them to be. Was the 'quarrel' perpetuated by its own wilfulness, by hardness of heart obscuring logic of the mind? Was it a rooted will to dispute and disown which chose the minutiae of polemic and ignored the critical 'theme in common' which wilful preoccupations of controversy neglected? On that 'theme in common' the whole case rests for 'a certain sympathy of Scriptures: Biblical and Quranic'. It will be well to state it first in order later to examine the heavy stakes in disputatious ways and means and see the odds the better in its light, and in what measure they remain.

That theme consists in the witness of both Scriptures to the 'caliphate of humankind' in the natural order which is basic to their world-view, their reading of the human situation. This sub-tenancy of the good earth under God, this managerial privilege learned and pursued in the physical world of space and time, are Allah's grant of 'dominion' or *khilafah* whereby we 'rule' *over* things by virtue of being *under* the sovereignty divine by which the situation holds good and endures. This is our 'double state' to which the Qur'an refers.[4] It is only rightly read and 'had' in both directions – ours to implement with genuine right as ever from, through and for the ultimate 'right' of Allah.

This means that human experience, in lively responsiveness to 'what we can do with what there is',[5] finds itself in a realm of means yielding to us a realm of ends, ends both furnishing and celebrating the mystery of being. Consciousness has the capacity to realize that we have been 'let be with a view to being'. There has been that *Kun fayakun* ('Be and there is') of the Qur'an, the 'Let there be' and the 'Let Us make' of the Bible. This scriptured perception of 'creation', in answering only the question Why?, leaves itself open to researchings around the kindred question How? Its confidence is that nothingness has been taken away, and here are we.

It remains within our option to make a churlish response that we are 'on our own', that the creation theme is our unprovable assertion or our wishful illusion. But, either way, avowal or disavowal are alike beyond 'proof'.[6] They will be decided only by trust or distrust. Bible and Qur'an invite and commend to us the former. They both see creation, creature-hood and prophethood as a firm triad of conviction – this 'dominion' entrusting the first to the second and that second (being so fragile, gullible, risk-prone) needing urgently to be 'educated' into its high dignity by dint of monitory, even minatory, legislation.[7] That threefold sequence is the clue to Semitic Scriptures and the Islamic *Shahadah*.[8]

The Hebrew Bible, whose 'let there be' embraces all humankind, narrows the custodianship by its 'chosen' 'land-and-people' covenant which makes the status of 'the Gentiles' somehow less intensely 'under God'. The New Testament firmly opens out, via its concept of redemptive grace, the initial inclusiveness of pre-Abrahamic order and ending the 'Gentile' distinction.

Thus all is inside the Quranic play on words, whereby *khaliqah* and *khalifah*, 'creature' and 'custodian', differ only by one letter and a single dot. The mission of the messengers, to guide, remind, exhort, enjoin and warn, tells the divine concern around the commission to us to belong, possess, develop, employ and engage the resources with which we are replenished by dint of our own intelligent response to the intelligibility 'nature' presents, the 'nature' that, while making no statements, will abundantly answer questions. To address the questions is the task of *khilafah*, the procedure of science and so, in the cumulative of history, the tale and toll of technology, the theme of civilizations. Allah has 'made us colonists' in the earth.[9]

This Biblical/Quranic reading of human *imperium* – its *over* earth but *under* heaven dual character – comes wonderingly in the question of Surah 7.172: 'Am I not your Lord?'[10] It is there in the crucial passage in Surah 2.30f, where Allah announces to the heavenly conclave of angels His intention to set a 'deputy' over the creation, an 'underling/overling', an Adamic progeny whom they are ordered to 'worship' in token that this status and dignity are by divine design, so that 'prostration' to him is 'submission' on their part to God.

When the angels demur, protesting that 'this is all folly', that the creature is unworthy of this high trust and will surely 'corrupt in the earth and shed blood', God maintains His purpose and tells them pointedly: 'I know what to you is unknown'. 'If there is 'risk' it is deliberately taken – a situation entirely in line with how the Qurʾan insists that creation and creaturehood are not a theme of 'jesting', nor an enterprise of futility.[11] They mean. They mean divinely because they mean humanly.

III

It is here in the unison of 'creation, creaturehood and prophethood' that we have the 'certain sympathy' of the Bible and the Qurʾan.[12] It consists in the two halves of the situation it describes, namely: 'There is a divine stake which God has invested *in* humankind, *and* via the given Scriptures God shares *with* them what He has staked *in* them.' The 'in' and the 'with' belong together. Given this non-jesting, non-futile world, it could not be that the Creator had no care for its issues or neglected the onus in the risks. Laws are futile without reckonings. To delegate must mean to monitor. The policy of entrusted creaturehood means a pattern of creaturely direction, or 'revelation' whereby the trustee may be minded aright. To delegate is to engage with the delegacy. Or, in Biblical idiom, 'the lord of the vineyard' has business with 'the husbandmen'. It could not be other-

wise with a 'serious' Creator letting be a serious earth in significant creaturely hands.[13]

Is it not this divine 'to' and 'with' the human role in the human scene
that the Scriptures belong and us humans with them? If we are on behalf
of God in our *khilafah*, then God is on behalf of us in the enablement of
guidance, *dhikr*, and all else His Scriptures afford us. Here the concept of
'signs' (*ayat*) tells this mutuality. Our sciences explore what nature signi-
fies (the intelligence/intelligibility exchange) but those same 'signs' also
summon the soul to celebration, to thankfulness, to veritable possession
via the arts of poetry, music and all else sensuous and joyous. For the New
Testament this is the sacramental principle for which 'all that is is holy'
yet still has to be handled so by genuine consecration. The *ayat* or 'verses'
of the Qur'an have the same role of alerting to a possessable world qua
technology *and* of inviting into a hallowing order of grateful appreciation.
Scripturally read, it is the same world which enables mathematicians,
engineers, technicians, that also prompts and inspires celebrants, musicians, artists, poets and – as the Christian would add – priests, applying
the word to all and sundry, seeing that 'every one has somewhat to offer'.[14]

This 'right handling', in which Allah via 'Scriptures' that enjoin and
exhort to it takes cognizance with us, does not 'just happen'. It has to be
resolutely willed, often against the grain of human carelessness or callous-
ness, our sorry negligence of consecration in what only desecrates.

That such is always the onus of the option that is ours in the will (or
the 'won't') stems clearly from the strange, yet vital, neutrality of the
realm of 'signs'. They are in our power to heed or neglect. We can indulge
in 'Newton's sleep' whether in spurning all that laboratories do, or in
despising the pleas to wonder and awe which nature makes incessantly to
heart and soul.[15] In that risk, laboratories are doubtless safer than sanc-
tuaries. But, whether heedful or heedless, the natural order will stay
securely rigorous.[16]

For plainly it does not discriminate between our attitudes to it. There
could be no moral, nor scientific, nor religious, order if it did. What Jesus
called the 'inclusiveness of rain on the just and the unjust'[17] is everywhere
present in how the natural order 'services' us and we align with it. It is
noteworthy, in our Scriptures, that the mandate to be and to possess
preceded any and every revelation for our guidance. All were subsequent
to and regulatory of its bestowal. We have to appreciate this genuinely
'secular' quality of the way things are. One does not have to be a Muslim
woman to become pregnant, nor a Christian man to initiate fatherhood.
There is no Buddhist aeronautics, no Hindu zoology, no Sikh biochem-
istry, no biologies for separatist sects. All faiths may propose different
attitudes and readings for these powers: their efficacy abides the same for
all.

It follows that in this sense of 'secular' (i.e. neutral about religion) we all concede – or accede – to be 'secular' to operate at all. Such is the very shape of the delegacy we have been given. We are only 'Muslim' or 'Christian' in the world in terms of whether we freely and truly 'consecrate' our usages, our sciences, our trades, our competences and our capacities and so our cultures according to the terms of our *khilafah* and/or as the sacramental order wherein we are cognizant of God as ever cognizant of us. Thus it takes our freedom to be 'submitted'. It is in our liberty to be – as God by the natural order confers it – that we are summoned to make our 'colonization' our deed of worship, our *imperium* our fealty.

It is noteworthy, not least in the Qur'an with its steady amazement about wombs and embryoes, that procreation looms so large in our *khilafah*. For only procreation keeps the creation generationally ongoing. And the mandate is never withdrawn. Such, post-Noah, was the Biblical assurance. The Lord 'who does not weary of mankind' by the same token sustains His trust in them. It is no small part of our deputyship that we give onwards in parenthood the same gift we first received in infancy. Thus even the continuity of the centuries is within our 'gift-in-trust'. 'Do you consider the seed you spill?' is the urgent question of Surah 56 along with three others about 'the earth you till, the water you drink and the fire you kindle'.[18]

IV

That fourth one, in our nuclear age of potential global self-destruction, is grimly contemporary. To reflect on it is to reach a further relevance of this Biblical/Quranic 'sympathy', not only of conviction about the 'caliphate of humankind' but also of acute anxiety. What has never been withdrawn has grown ever more loaded both with menace and with liberation. We exult in emancipations, in standards of living, in magnified amenities, that the accumulation of techniques has granted us, far beyond the imagination or the cognizance of our forebears. Yet we perceive them beset by desperate injustices, harsh inequalities, and haunted by dark shadows of foreboding. The common doctrine of the divine stake *in* us as also – thanks to scriptured revelation – shared *with* us, surely becomes ever more bonding between us by virtue of its increasing urgency in the here and now. The more awesome our prospects of where we have arrived, the more awesome the summons of what our mandate was divinely willed to be. For our only sanity, our one salvation, is to know and own it for the thing it is, a 'dominion'/*khilafah* which waits uncoercively for our will to an *islam*. That we are genuinely 'entrusted' is proven in the divine fidelity to an order of things where non-*islam*, despite all the magnanimity enabling otherwise, can be our verdict.

That we are in crisis has always been the case. So much is evident from the implications of Genesis 1 and 2, or the Qur'an's Surahs 2 and 7 and all we have reviewed there – creation, creaturehood and prophethood in their single relevance. That the crisis is more loaded than it has ever been is evident enough. Because it is so, we encounter another element in this 'certain sympathy'. It takes us to the theme often to the fore in current Muslim apologetic that there is in Islam a *Da'wah*, a summons, a mission even, it must bring to the West – to a West it perceives as astray, in the grip of delusion and 'the secular', lost in the wrongness of any search to be found.

Christians traditioned to think of 'mission' in the opposite direction may find this thesis odd. But it deserves careful respect. That all is not well with the West is obvious enough, but what is 'not well about it' is not likely to heed the likely form of positive Islamic remedying advice or image. It will not 'heal the hurt' because it has not fathomed it. Nor will its religious downrightness win it a sophisticated hearing. Yet is has much to underline in the common theme we have explored, a theme its Christian mentors have always known and loved. They need Muslim community in effectively possessing it now, with provisos we have yet to see.

For though Christianity may seem, to Muslims, to be 'failed religion' at least in respect of its western territory, the factors lie in a gathering western lapse of confidence in the human situation as truly a delegacy from Allah, meant for human self-realizing by due exercise of 'caliphate'. The factors have been many, making for perceptions of 'The Wasteland',[19] or a wearied 'boredom' as from an inescapable futility. People have arrived where 'they no longer believe in belief'. There are no more grand metaphysical systems, no more metahistorical narratives any more on which we can dependably rely. The age of great doctrinal confidences are at an end.

Further, notions of the role of language have undermined a trust in 'texts' at all, still more 'the holy ones'. These should never rightly be exempt from normal doubt and scrutiny and if they plead to be they are the more undone. There is no construct of faith which may not be 'deconstructed' so as to forfeit all authority. As a cynic had it: 'the Lord created the world out of nothing, and now the nothingness is showing through.' Religious belief-systems are devices for conjuring up a sense of solace which, realistically, can only be false and illusory. We cannot verify what we may not falsify and we can dependably do neither with 'God and His gift of caliphate'.

Further, there has been a measure of intoxication about what science has achieved, multiplying devices and fuelling desires to bring all things effectively under its feet. It is evident that developments in techniques have set the pace and controlled the patterns of change more than religions have, or ever will be able to re-order or control. Those techniques have all too often been driven by political control or military power that tend to leave sober hopefuls in despair about any human amenability to 'common good' morally discerned and served. Though much in fact in scientific advance has been owed to imaginative intuition more than sheer experiment, science tends to indulge in self-idolatry as 'mastering' all else rather than being itself 'mastered' inside a religiously known 'caliphate' under God.[20]

And further again, these items of potential despair and/or of recession in the public sense of God or 'final truth' are all, for many minds today, accentuated by the sorry panorama of religions. These too often seem, systems of mental tyranny, citadels of obscurantism or bigotry, apt at the subjugation of the social order to their will, and compromisers of human dignity, male and female. How well do they order their own selves by their best lights, how badly by their worst? In fear for themselves, they have too often conspired against the divine mandate to be 'secular' as if, inside 'caliphate' it was not present in the very summons to be 'under God'.

It follows that the Muslim mind, in any will to 'help the West', must itself wrestle with this contemporary malaise from which the West suffers. For it is everywhere present and growing and Islam has no immunity from its inroads or its challenge. Echoes of 'the Wasteland' actual or latent, run through the prose and poetry of Muslim communities – Arab, Turkish, Urdu, Malay – alike in East and West. The Islamic diaspora in Europe and the Americas shares the factors directly. They are ubiquitous on every *qiblah* to Mecca, or in every would-be Medina of the Islamic state. Muslims can only aid the West if they too wrestle with the same *fitnah* of modernity in the radical measure it deserves.[21]

For, by the common doctrine of our 'caliphate', we only have it when we recognize and undertake its terms. It is never ours by absence of mind or insouciance, but only by deliberate response. What is in trust turns upon our grasp of being entrusted. The malaise we have reviewed has happened by defaulting on its own significance. The renewing of divine worship hinges on the re-discovery of human dignity, of our liability to be as those who have been 'let be' by divine will and for divine ends.

It is just the absence of this recognition of God and the divinely given human dignity that explains the attitudes in the West that Muslims so resent and dispute – the cultural arrogance, the near-satiated consumerism, the blatant materialism, the over-indulged world of gross advertising and the consequent neglect of others' poverty, the crude imbalance of the world's economies. All these are symptoms of an abeyance of the will to worship and of the capacity for wonder. They go along with a forfeiture of sexual modesty and personal reticence, with a cult of bravado and the tireless quest for pseudo-satisfactions in the media or the drug culture.

When taken in its true significance, this malaise is not to be relieved merely by being accused or deplored, unless the 'disputanda' begin from an honest encounter with the factors from which it stemmed, a right pursuance of the religious dimensions of its correction and redemption. The post First World War 'secularity', for example, of the Atatürk Revolution, was too abrupt and irreligious to avail that long-standing Islamic culture. It is little wonder that Islam has renewed itself in the aftermath so painfully and partially. For the problems the story generated were not faced in the themes of Ziya Gökalp about Islam as a mere veneer for a Turkism on which it may lay an incidental imprint.[22]

Given that many in the West are aware of their predicament and that there is potential 'sympathy' between a Christian and an Islamic 'scripturehood', does not the situation bid us bring that right diagnosis of our ills to work on their correction, to forego a churlish scepticism about our human being and its meaning as these belong, for us all, in the will of Allah to be caring party to them in the fidelity of His creating mind? If so, there are two remaining duties of 'preface and precaution'.

V

The first must be some notice of the long, often polemical distrust of, or attack upon, the other's Scripture. 'Preface' has thus far left this aspect aside as not one to impede the broad inter 'sympathy' we must see as central. Can we leave polemic to the margins where it belongs? There will doubtless always be those who will to stay polemical, denunciatory and 'quarrelsome' on their own querulous terms. So 'precaution' is needed lest our whole enterprise be clamoured out of court.

The conviction here is that it is saner to keep with the salient theme of divine–human 'entrustment to these entrusted' as not only the urgent terms for contemporary technology but also the clearest loyalty to a scriptural authority. Even so, there are scholarly obligations each community of faith has to its hallowed texts, some of which are faced here in Chapter 6. It is wiser that they handle their own, without traditional denigration of the other.

Hebraic and Christian animosity to the Qur'an goes back to strictures against those faiths inside the Quranic text itself, notably in Medinan Surahs when Muhammad's eager anticipation of recognition by older 'people of the Book' proved to be disappointed. Resentment could then become mutual and engender controversy as to whether Muhammad's coming had not been foretold in Biblical text, so that an alleged silence meant that the text had been 'corrupted' or perverted. Controversy then tended to breed upon itself with dispute about the meaning of *paracletos* in John's Gospel.[23]

Tahrif any way was alleged in other areas to square the Qur'an's doctrine of consensus with all other valid Scriptures, given evident disparities with these as their versions stood. Then there was the tangle about 'abrogation' (*naskh*) and how it might operate inside the Qur'an and in what form it could obtain for issues between them. Beyond the minutiae of such issues, there has always been the partisan animus which underlay them, wherein on either side there was the will to prevail, to score points and clinch their own case. Inasmuch as this animus engendered what it contested, making the controversies what they were, it could only prove religiously barren, an exercise in mutual alienation.

Both scripturaries, over long centuries, had to endure what they received from the other, in terms of *dhimmi*-inferiorization, military conquest – whether by *Jihad* or Crusade, the retaliations of the centuries in the Arab East, Anatolia, Spain, the Balkans, Egypt and North Africa and beyond the Sahara, the Sudan and Nubia. These legacies, held in persistent memories, religiously fortified to brood on them, surely suggest and require a readiness now to abide one another by conceding either to the other what their 'people' take their 'Books' to be and leave to *their* integrity whatever critique they see them to need. There is no compromise in so doing, if we mean to relate to each other and to where we all now are in a global humankind in unprecedented crisis about its meaning and its destiny, the mind of its peace.[24]

By that measure we reach our final duty. It is to ponder our thesis and theme as to Biblical/Quranic divine stake *in* us as being also divinely shared *with* us, both measures being crucial, either to other. Despite all urging to the contrary, 'we are not on our own'.[25] We are divinely commissioned 'to be' and 'to occupy' but 'under God' and in delegacy for Him. Neither are we 'on our own' in the discharge of our 'trust' in time and place. By the 'education' of 'revelation' we are not in some limbo of 'ignorance' about how to fulfil our 'office' as sub-president servants of Allah.

What is crucial between us, recipients alike of 'office' and of 'guidance', is how far this 'sharing' goes? Is the guiding revelation one of law alone, of what will be scriptured as calligraphic text? Or might it be 'incarnational' in order to be redemptive? In which case the Scripture from it would be more than codal, textual and verbal but also biographical, housed in a history which written texts would only enshrine as a 'language' more ultimate than themselves, 'the Word made flesh', read in the distinctive character of the New Testament, its Gospels and its Letters. Its logic belongs with how amenable we might ever be to divine employ, how apt for the sufficing of verbal education, how liable to see our *imperium* as neither trust nor privilege but only an illusion round our loneliness.[26]

'Acceptance' of 'the let-be' over against such usurpation has to be the care and study of the chapters that follow, with the precaution that keeps in mind this essential disparity between our Scriptures. It is one that belongs with our distinctive 'esteems' of God.[27]

Chapter 1

Divine Ends Set in Human Means – Creation and Cosmos

I

THE MUSLIM'S *SHAHADAH* or 'confession of faith' has an admirable brevity well able, for example, to be fitted on to the Saudi Arabian flag. It would be an odd idea to imagine either of the classic Christian creeds being legible in so small a space. Yet, belonging squarely as it does with the human world, its very brevity needs serious amplification for which we must draw on the Qur'an itself. Workable creeds always imply more than they can conveniently contain or, rather, what they contain pre-supposes or significantly suggests what they do not expressly say. So it is urgently with the Islamic seven words: *La ilaha illa Allah*, 'There is no deity except God: *Muhammadun Rasul-Allah*, Muhammad is the Messenger of God.'

The words are terse, emphatic and declamatory and, precisely in being so, enfold a world within that 'colon'[1] between its two clauses. That 'Allah is One and there is none but He' has to be stated in this negating form because the initial hearing and setting were beset with plural concepts of tribal gods presiding over diverse aspects of human experience in a harsh environment inured to adversity and hence much liable to superstitious anxieties and this-world palliatives – a society whose poetic tradition was burdened with a sense of mortal brevity and the elusiveness of life.[2]

Allah, alone, in over-ruling unity of unrivalled sovereignty was thus the positive liberation that required to be told in that negative *la* – the *la* in Arabic of absolute negation denying to all pseudo entities any title to human worship or credence. The *Shahadah* was all inclusive about what it disallowed, eliminating all that might clog or cloud the pagan soul with the unreal and the illusory, from which came haunting tyrannies of fear and social pathos. In context, that negative formula was its supreme glory as well as its necessary duty.

Yet so to realise is to be led to ponder the implications in the situation that required it. In another, perhaps a modern context, there would be point in asking: Why should the unity of God need such insistent assertion – assertion in this negative shape? Why, in short, does *Allahu akbar* need to be said: 'God is greater!'? What is hindering God from being God, that we have to go on affirming it? From where is the challenge coming if, in truth, there are no other deities? Should not the unity, the reality, of Allah be somehow inviolate, beyond all necessity of mere human asseveration? Indeed, is not the inviolability of Allah something utterly instinctive to the Islamic mind and faith? Can it really be that 'God has to be *let be*' by us humans whom He has created?

Answer has to be that, despite the eternal security of the divine Reality beyond all human 'approval' or 'cognisance', nevertheless that eternal Reality has to be 'conceded' such by human 'submission', human adoration, human *islam*. Otherwise, 'He who is' – in all our thoughts – 'is not', as a Hebrew psalmist said of all who lived in studied indifference to Him.[3] We have somehow to understand that in the very nature of 'the Indubitable', 'God only and divinely Himself', there is this self-risking quality whereby His sovereignty requires recognition. 'Requires' must (and can only) have the double sense of 'demands' and 'awaits', 'claims' and 'needs', from human hearts and hands.

So much is in the silence at the core of the *Shahadah*. If it were not so there would be no point to *islam*. That *la ilaha* proves that idolatry happened – and happens. Idolatries occur and need to be denied. There is a pluralism that has to be denounced. The God Who is has to be the God He is, and we humans are such as to have that 'submission' in our option. The Qur'an refers often to humans existing *min duni-Illahi*, 'to the exclusion of God'.[4] To be sure, even such 'move and live and have their being' in the inclusion which is His creation, but do so in deliberate insouciance, until a summons out of it arrests them.

That imperative, never silent and, the *Shahadah* believes, made ultimate in Islam, arrives in the second clause which concerns the ultimate 'apostolate of Muhammad.' Its form by Arabic laws make him '*the* apostle', the ultimate member of a long sequence that culminates and ends with him.[5] But that second clause waits like the first, on things it does not say. Why messengers at all? To whom sent and for what intent? About 'letting God be God' obviously (in view of that first clause) – but where is this done and by whom, in what arena and for what ends?

Plainly the silent *Shahadah* infers the whole created order, this cosmos of the physical/spiritual which is our human territory, the realm of our 'dominion'. It is to the Qur'an we must go for the 'things credal' the *Shahadah* silently comprises but which are no less part of its central conviction about the human scene as a trust divinely located, entrusted and assigned in human hands so that *in media res*, in living history, in cultures and sciences, in arts and societies, God might be 'let be' in the manifold *mise-en-scène* of our earthly creaturehood.

The 'humanism' of the Qurʾan – if in this sense we may use the term – has often been explored.[6] It is the defining theme of the apostolate of Muhammad. For only to a responsible creaturehood would, or should, messengers be sent. Messengers with no missives would be vacuous and their missives more so without recipients carrying responsibility for the concrete situation all the behests, warnings, reminders and directives concerned. Without such creaturehood, prophethoods would be point-less. Mandates are only to the mandated and these are the human tenants and delegated custodians of the good earth as a realm of 'signs' suited to answer their intelligence and so yield the economic and social orders of history for which they are liable – and all under God, where we humans are 'let be to let God be' as bearing the trust He confers.

All this is the celebratory theme of the Qurʾan. One pivotal passage is Surah 2.30f, where the Lord announces in heavenly conclave the appoint-ment of a *khalifah* in the earth. The terms as noted in the Preface are intended to coincide.[7] We humans, precisely in all our faculties in a phys-ical setting tuned to their employ, are 'on behalf of Allah' as those, whence all cultures flow. When the angels in conclave immediately suspect the wisdom in making 'sub-agents' out of fickle humans, Allah remains unde-terred, having His own counsel and the risks it augurs. Instead of not venturing, not 'letting us be', those sceptics are promptly ordered to 'pros-trate to' the creature in recognition of what divine things are now at stake in him.[8]

There can be no doubt for readers of the Qurʾan that this human dignity constitutes a profound divine intention due to be fulfilled in the human domain. This is corroborated not only by its stress on nature as a realm of 'signs' set to be cognised by human percipience (thanks to the equip-ment of the senses) enabling a mastery of the physical realm, sufficient to undergird the whole structure of civilisation and sustain it through a cumulative history. It is symbolised by the creature's competence with 'the names' of things – a skill that is the foundation of the sciences.[9]

It is further confirmed by the insistence the Qurʾan lays on the 'seri-ousness' divinely enshrined in the whole enterprise of a creation for the sake of creaturehood and of a creaturehood for the sake of creation. Surahs 21.16 and 44.38 insist that 'God has not created the heaven and the earth and all between as if He acted in jest.' For, as the exegete Al-Baidawi observed, 'it is freighted with all kinds of wonders'. Humans do not serve or learn 'a jesting creation'. 'Do you think that We have created you in vain?' (or pointlessly) Surah 23.115 enquires. Muslims like Christians, but unlike so minded Buddhists, do not have to suspect the world, and all that is, as some kind of confidence-trick of which we should be wary, or as a snare by which we might be deluded, a trap in which we

3

might be caught. Quite the contrary, the world means, holds significant wonder, deserves awe, incites to reverence and enlists energies it will repay. For nature is that kind of dominion, underwriting the chemist, the engineer, the peasant at the plough, the tactitian in the laboratory. Or, in Biblical language, it is clearly a 'dominion' where lively, intelligent, percipient and so grateful humanism properly belongs. The Muslim would want to say of his mosque – as even a poet half-agnostic could find it in himself to say of a church: 'A serious on serious earth it it . . . fit to grow wise in.'[10] The 'wisdom' latent in that 'seriousness' is the very crux of the history of the world and the human *mise-en-scène* itself.

II

But, 'where', as the Bible asks, 'is wisdom to be found' (Proverbs 28:12)? As the angels anticipated, creaturehood is loaded with risk. The odds against human success in divine service, in reverent agency in the divine behalf, are heavy. For the creature is fickle, frail, forgetful, even obdurate and perverse, capable of wilful 'wronging' both of the self and of the world.

Hence the mission of the messengers, to inform of dignity, to inculcate the norms and educate the discharge of stature implicit in the very trust of it and in the strange adventurous magnanimity of Allah. Thus, having filled in the vacant data in the heart of the *Shahadah*, its two clauses cohere in one – a Oneness violated by idolatry and a mission calculated to reinstate that Oneness by bringing the wisdom of a final revelation.[11] All holds together – creaturehood and prophethood in crucial inter-association, the purpose of divine ends brought home to their setting in the human means.

The missive/mission theme in this explicit bond with an Islamic humanism needs to be taken up more intensively in Chapter 2. Meanwhile it is evident enough how in this 'seriously empowered' creaturehood we have a manifest sympathy of Biblical and Quranic scriptures, a common mind around what in the one is 'dominion' and is equally in the other *khilafah*. Both nouns, the Latin and the Arabic, tell of a warrant to 'have charge' over a cosmos yielding into human hands a significant *imperium* wherein and whereby to be fulfilled in the very art of being human, vested – as that art is – in the senses and their skills in intelligent employ.

Celebratory psalms in the Hebrew and the Arabic have a congenial feel.[12] Doubtless, there are differences stemming from the nature of the terrain. A Palestinian terraced vineyard does not compete with some palm-ringing Arabian oasis, nor the yield of the one with the solace of the other. Biblical rains are more generous than the rare Arab brief and transitory greening of the earth where infrequent showers fall. Yet the steady urge of both Scriptures to gratitude and 'recalling of the Name of the Lord' belongs to either equally. *Shukr* is a salient theme in the Qur'an's tuition and becomes the very antonym of *kufr* – that 'unbelief' that lacks all cognisance of debt to God.[13] Where theology is rooted in doxology there is hope that its more divisive strains can allow some consanguinity.

The Bible's intense Hebraic focus may present an obstacle. For the Qur'an's perception of human husbandry of the good earth – while holding its own Arabia is high esteem – is symptomatic of all human tenancies. But the obstacle is not insuperable. The elements of Hebraic destiny, i.e. ancestry, territory and history, the who, where and whence of their identity, are universal denominators of human life by birth, habitat and story, as racial, territorial and social. Thus Hebraic self-perceived exceptionality was – it is fair to say – exceptional only in its intensity, an intensity which can be seen, in turn, as an education for all identities. Was not Amos sure that all peoples had their migrations, their exodus and their entry (Amos 9:7)? In that event 'the men of Judah are His pleasant plant' (Isaiah 5:7) may be of universal import concerning all 'plantings of the Lord by which He might be glorified' (Isaiah 61:3). This hope need not be annulled by the deep animus against the Hebraic heritage which developed in the Medinan Qur'an out of a confrontation that had nothing to do with human tenancy and tillage. For these are universal dimensions of all human experience.

There are two features common to both Biblical and Quranic doxologies and hymnologies, namely deep acknowledgement of nurture via fertility and a perceptive mind to take due mental stock of an amazing world. Given their deep theological assurances of verbal revelation, Semitic minds may have been less inquisitive or investigative than the Greek mind, with its instinct for philosophy exploring mind with mind in the Socratic garden. For the Greek deities were such as to prompt intelligence to ignore them. Yahweh and Allah, enthroned over the Semitic scene, were of a different order – awesome, sovereign and transcendent, creating, governing and strangely delegating privilege into human keeping. Precisely in doing so, Semitic Lordship made room for total wonder in a world of total dependence and these both enabled and evoked a hymning of human experience no Greek mythologies could conjure from their pluralists.

Hence the Qur'an's impulse to kindle the praise of Allah with a reiterated *wa* of invocation: 'By the chartered winds . . .' (77.1), 'By the heaven and the night star . . .' (86.1). The arresting phenomena of external nature are the summons to awaken praise in having already seized on the imagination. To take stock would be prosaic, mercenary reaction. Only an ever incisive vigilance does rightly by the intense mystery of things.

In this quality the Qur'an, with all that is properly its unique character, is deeply akin to the Hebrew psalmist saluting the Lord 'who stretches out the heavens like a curtain' and 'makes the clouds His chariot, walking upon the wings of the wind' (104.2–3). He uses a personal address while the Qur'an would shrink from saying: 'O my soul,' 'O Lord my God.'[14] Yet the awareness breathes the same music, the same register of wonder.

This sublime poetry, however, in both cases, is prosaically aware of 'daily bread'. 'Green herb for the service of man' (Psalm 104:14) is the Biblical; 'the earth is dotted with adjacent fields, with farms and vineyards and clumps of palms' says the Qur'an (13.4). Both, in their different idiom, are aware of the precariousness of daily living, the onset of 'scarcity', the failure of vital waters and the vagaries of winds and tides. They celebrate a cosmos which ministers to human need, by day and night, by toil and sleep, by sun and moon or stars in orbits, by irrigating rivers and sequential seasons, 'making glad – or apprehensive – the heart of man'. Theirs is an unashamed 'anthropocentrism' received as a divine benefaction but only on the ground of an unfailing reverence and a perpetual thanksgiving.

This perennial cognisance of debt in the Biblical/Quranic human cosmos is informed by a studied reckoning of mind with mind. 'When I consider Thy heavens, the work of Thy hands' is its familiar cry, and the words that follow: 'What is man that You are mindful of him?' are not craven or sceptical but, rather, a genuine surprise that 'You prize him so highly'. This mutual 'consideration'[15] of the divine for the human, of the human for the divine, means in either case a habit of esteem – that of Allah vested in our creaturehood; ours trained upon His handiwork.

The latter is graphically told in four questions in Surah 56.58, 63, 68 and 71. 'And have you seen?', as the Preface earlier noted, the four elements that are human sexuality, human tillage, human watering and human fire. The invitation is to reflection around those four basics of birth, earth, water and fire. 'Do you consider . . .' might be the best translation of 'seeing and having a view of'. The logic in sexual procreation, in agriculture, irrigation and combustion not only argues our total dependence on facts entirely given and from them doings for which we are liable. It constrains us to glorify God in the very physicality of body, land and earth's amenities with a duly responsive mind.

How close this 'considering' in Surah 56 is to the Wisdom tradition in the Biblical Proverbs and kindred Ecclesiasticus and The Wisdom of Ben Sirach. It tells a cognisance fit to nurture those 'who maintain the fabric of the world' and 'in whose craft is their prayer'. Ezekiel, even in his animus against Tyre, could duly appreciate the celebration of her products, the manifold elegance of her merchandise, her mariners, her pilots and her boundless commerce. Had she not once furnished the very Temple in Jerusalem? Magnificence would wait even on her ruin.

Whether or not in hallowing hands, this world of inviting intelligibility is, for the Semitic mind, made amenable to human intelligence. Options – of investigation tending to a mastery – are ours because the physical and material realm is patterned to serve us by the option-less 'laws' of its chemistry, its physics, its biology, its functions at large.[16] Doubtless there are hazards, but these 'dependables', discernible everywhere and waiting to be understood and harnessed, yield themselves to our *khilafah* and underwrite the economic order on which culture and society are built. There was for the psalmist this divine 'handiwork' furnishing our human 'handicraft' by the very nature of the opportunity it affords to us. The natural order has this measure of a non-volitional *islam*, a conformity to law that enables a mastery of ours, to be in turn the realm of our *islam* by act of conscious will.

Thus the Qur'an throughout is calling for intelligent awareness and occupation of the mortal scene, with its legible 'signs' and its accessible 'names'. We have been 'let be' to 'make be' alike in gratitude and industry, in the dignity of a generous trust. There is that frequent word *la'alla* in the Qur'an, the great 'perhaps' with a number of verbs it governs, like *La'allakum ta'qilun*, 'perhaps you may use your wits', or *La'allakum tatafakkarun*, 'perhaps you may think hard'. In Surah 36.45 the phrase uses the verb *turhamun* 'perhaps you may be mercied' (passive) in a context referring to 'signs' or 'tokens' from your Lord. Whatever the Biblical Obadiah (17) meant by his 'Israel possessing possessions' in his immediate context, the language must surely include all humans moving in the world of responsive order and taking in hand the amenities it presents. Frequently elsewhere in the Qur'an the *la'alla* form is used with the third person pronoun attached – 'perhaps they . . .'.

What is noteworthy about *la'alla* is that almost invariably it occurs with the plural verb. Our contemporary world needs to remember that so much in these defining Scriptural societies was corporate and collective, sharply tribal and local. Our sort of individualism needs to appreciate a quite contrasted temper in 'possessing possessions' only by dint of the pagan order or the communal culture that left little to personal will.

Even so the basic Biblical/Quranic principle of human 'dominion' in, and from, a natural setting answering its skills, pervades their world. Moreover, the Semitic faith in a single Creator and a dignified creaturehood liberated the otherwise pagan mind from the tyranny of a multiplicity of forces operating – and intimidating – inside a partial chaos not yet read as a cosmos. For all the powerful tribalism of Muhammad's Meccan scene, there is no mistaking the incidence, via the Qur'an, of personal, even private, initiatives in which the self could be free of the tribe.[17] The Qur'an is quite emphatic about personal liability, insisting that 'no soul bears any burden but its own' and only our own deeds are morally assessable.[18] If this would exclude the vicarious – as surely it never can – there can be no doubting or eluding the onus of our single personhood as Quranically perceived.

The Biblical tradition, in its long pre-occupation with the historical and the episodic, and with its intensely collective consciousness, has more occasion for the emergence of personal singularity. The Qur'an, by contrast, owes much of its weightedness to the single persona of Muhammad. In either case, there is no weightier validation of the role of selfhood, in its singularity, than the vocation of 'the prophet', the spokesman for the Eternal. He even becomes, as with Jeremiah and 'the suffering servant', the single individual who carries the destiny of the entire people, who enshrines in lonely fidelity the vocation even of an apostate population.

In the different context of the Qur'an Muhammad too is the pivotal, the definitive figure, 'the best of Muslims', in whom – as well as via whom – human potentials are most fully realised by virtue of his summons into prophethood. That summons, however, for all its idiosyncratic character, may be read as the surest token of what can be divinely entrusted into human toil and care and loyalty. So, in however exalted a way, it stands also as betokening what it also educates, namely the tenure on the good earth of *all* its peasants, farmers, traders, merchants, technicians – indeed all denizens – all 'handicrafters' amid this 'handiwork of the Lord'.

III

The course of thought is hereby led to a theme right at the core of this 'sympathy of Scriptures' concerning 'divine ends vested in human means'. It is the theme the Preface raised which has long confused Muslim/Christian discourse, namely the issue of what we ambiguously dub 'the secular'.

It must follow from all the foregoing about 'divine ends entrusted into human means' that 'the secular' exists. It exists precisely in the fact that 'dominion'/*khilafah* granted to us leaves us in a veritable option as to whether we will – or we will not – conform our acts and deeds to the divine purpose. Only so is there any point, substance or reality, in the claim on us to be *muslim*, i.e. to behave in the trust of things according to Allah's design concerning them, thus placed into our hands. If that conformity, that *islam*, were somehow automatic, mechanically assured, inevitable, enforced or imposed, there need be no urgent appeal for it. There need be no Islam, no Muhammad in vital prophethood enjoining it, in the event there was nothing left to us to do or will or think or resolve. Only the liable need prophets: only the free can heed them.

Thus the entire thrust of Biblical or Quranic Scripture is that 'the secular' is there – there in the option of *khilafah*, there in the presentation to our intelligence of an intelligible world we are invited to inhabit and take up in act and will. There is no 'obedience' that is not willed and it is nowhere willed if it cannot be withheld. Idolatry happens – as is evident enough in both Scriptures. Elijahs and Muhammads, not to say Salihs, Shu'aibs and Huds, denounce it. They could have neither missives nor missions if *shirk*, our defiance of God, the will to say 'no', did not exist. The whole *raison d'être* of the Qur'an dissolves if its 'guidance', its 'reminder', its 'warning' have no hearers for whom they could signify in a free and concrete situation – the situation we have examined. Even blasphemy can happen or it need not be reproved. That 'only God is God' requires to be said because the contrary is alleged, assumed or sinfully desired. Only if our 'caliphate' is real can law or prophet mean.

The problem here – and the confusion – stem from a cast of mind which wants to suspect that the 'dominion'/*khilafah* is unreal, as if the Lord who granted it had somehow withdrawn it – of which there is no evidence at all but rather awesome evidence to the contrary. Why should we posit some 'change' with Allah, some loss of nerve, some turn-about unworthy of His name?[19] Our creaturehood is vested in a divine Self-consistency. We are 'let be' to 'let His will be' by and in us, with His world insofar as His design in creaturehood has left this to us. Only in that situation do the very Scriptures belong. The human 'conditionality' of His will is by that very will itself as 'the Creator of this creaturehood'. So far Surah 2.30f and numerous other passages.[20]

To think rightly of the divine stake and purpose in the human privilege and still have in right view Allah's transcendent sovereignty, we need to see how this *de facto* 'secular' is nevertheless still inside a *de jure* Lordship. That has been axiomatic from the start, in that the *de facto* order of things was deliberately within the *de jure* power. There is nowhere doubt of what we may call the *essential* sovereignty of God, the unchallenged reign of the divine Being. On every Biblical/Quranic premise about creation, however, this *essential* sovereignty encompasses a subordinate capacity which is ours in humanness. What proceeds under the latter, being humanly at issue, comes under the former in terms of law and revelation, of prophet mission and guidance and grace – these being the uncompulsive-ness with which omnipotence wills to move. Willing it so is the very soul of the meaning in the cry: *Allahu akbar*. We worship an Omnipotence with the magnanimity to make us responsible for ends both His and ours.

Thus what we call 'the secular' has to be understood as a potential for 'the sacred' but at our hands. That it is only 'hallowed' (never automatically) by human will and hand does not mean, or imply, that it has ever been outside the divine rule.[21] It means simply that the divine has willed it this way, since 'there is no (there cannot be) compulsion in religion' (Surah 2.255). To recognise 'the secular' as the very destiny of 'the sacred' – a destiny made to turn upon *our* will – is to understand the very reason for Islam. Nothing is, or was ever, outside the domain of Allah as some realm where He had no rule, no power, no place. His ever being Lord over all things has to be through our human *islam* in all those realms which

9

His being Lord has assigned to our 'caliphate'. Divine omnipotence was, and is, of that 'caliphatising' order, sovereign alike in so willing and so providing – where the whole relevance of Semitic Scriptures comes into its own. There is, indeed, 'None but He,' God over all, in all, and through all.

The 'secular/sacred' distinction – more familiar to Christian tradition – is in no way, then, alien to the Qur'an's world, however difficult it has been to 'get' the term in Arabic.[22] We can usefully pursue the argument via the Christian sense of 'sacrament', as 'minding for holy'. All faiths tell the spiritual in the physical and thanks to its Christology, Christianity is the most sacramental of all. But the theme is latent, not only in the evident physical element in Muslim prayer and pilgrimage but also in the whole Quranic concept of 'signs', integral to all that obtains between sentient humans and the natural order.[23] The same 'signs' which arrest some scientist and so enable and equip the 'dominion' they offer, must also address the devout and kindle them to gratitude. It is no small part of a 'sacramental' reality, that where the crafts and trades and techniques arise, the arts, the poets, the musicians also kindle. Where we exploit we must also consecrate, where we attain to master we must also celebrate with hallowing.

This 'sacramental' principle may well be uncongenial to the mind of Islam but it chimes well with this doctrine of 'signs' everywhere awaiting reverent cognisance from humankind. Given Islam's suspect, or even hostile, attitude towards Christian liturgical rituals around the hallowing of the material order ('Here we offer and present . . . ') this sense of 'the secular into the sacred' may be a very tenuous sympathy, given also the Qur'an's ambivalence about 'priesthood' in care of such rituals.[24] Nevertheless, it cannot be denied that here is a 'sympathy' between Scriptures. An ancient Christian formula, 'The things of God for people of God', can well translate into an Islamic doctrine of things humanly in trust within Allah's created order of commodities transacting in communities.[25] Each faith in its own idiom is only taking seriously the 'serious' business of our creaturehood, our role *over* things ever *under* God – and those things only truly under God when we are rightly over them. Such was, such is, *khilafah*, with 'dominion'. It is significant that there is no mention of 'caliphs' in the Qur'an who are rulers, emperors, kings, potentates or sultans (with the casual exception of David).[26] The only *khulafa'* the Qur'an knows (plural of *khalifah)* are the common folk of daily life.

IV

This 'hallowing' of things mundane so that they belong by our conscious intent with the rule and reign of God – insofar as these, as we have seen, are left to us – might well be deemed an 'islamizing' of the natural order and of the economic realm it yields. The coined term is exactly right as understood, here, not in respect of government under a 'powered religion' (an issue to which we have to come later) but rather an essential, practical piety of *muslim* wills in the dailiness of life. As such it means the *taqwa*, or inherent 'piety', that essentially defines Islam, which Fazlur Rahman counts central to his *Major Themes of the Qur'an*.[27] Of frequent reference in the Qur'an, *taqwa* is the supreme 'virtue' by which we ward off evil and recognize that the ultimate criterion – being outside ourselves in God's order – locates us *under* obligation to which we are for ever accountable. It is the essential 'fear of God' summoned to a right handling of a world where Allah's *qadar*, or 'measure' of things, is precisely what enables those 'dependables' on which, as we saw earlier, all life depends. That sort of 'necessity', which makes, for example, for chemistry, calculus, anatomy, medicine, engineering and all the rest – these being material and non-volitional – has its counterpart in the obligatoriness of the volitional conduct which *taqwa* obeys and which, by obeying, protects (a part meaning of the term) from vagary, evil and that 'corrupting in the earth' the angels so feared.

Such *taqwa* holds us to 'the limits' it ordains or – better – recognizes and obeys. Thus,

Human nature . . . becomes endowed with that quality which renders it 'service to God' (*'ibadah*).[28]

There is an open question around whether *taqwa* is rightly called 'conscience'. Certainly it is a restraining and constraining factor keeping the self within 'the bounds' Allah has decreed.

It must be obvious at once how crucially *taqwa* bears on contemporary issues of environment, pollution and a 'God-fearing' ecology. A lively sense of 'trusteeship' of the planet has the vexing burden of how it is made effective in an ever competitive, money-motivated world. What may be viable as *taqwa*/ 'conscience' in the private domain becomes intensely far-to-seek in the collectives of nations, hemispheres, interests and corporate operations.

The deep irony also is that religions can so readily become one of these – a vested interest of punditry and 'official guardians' of dogma or *Shari'ah* who may 'transgress all bounds' in the very claim to 'protect' them. Serving God with authority resolves all too frequently and tragically into serving authority instead of God, in that lust of power which cannot acknowledge or renounce its own mischievous perversity. Here are burdens we must defer to Chapter 7.

Meanwhile, any 'sympathy' thus far explored between two Scriptures and their communities of centuries, must recognize that the Islamic mind finds peculiar difficulty in reading our human *khilafah* in its authentic

Quranic dimensions of 'Allah let be' by and in our human entrustedness with creaturehood in such authentic terms. It seems to collide impossibly with the Muslim esteem of divine omnipotence utterly uninvolved with such compromising associations, an omnipotence essentially reserving all power, all will, to itself, as – and only so – *qadir ʿala kulli shay*, 'almighty over all things', the ever humanly untrammelled, 'exalted above all that ye associate'. How then can He have anything so staked in us, opting for 'association' with our finitude.

Truly the tensions run deep and bear constantly on the text of the Qurʾan. They are very different tensions from those which belong with the Hebrew Bible and its exclusive Hebraic 'covenant' between this Yahweh and this 'His people'. Islam reverts to the Noahid 'pledge' of nature sustaining humankind and 'the rainbow in the cloud'. That habitat/inhabitant equation belongs diversely with all peoples. It has to be read as a summons, an invitation into the manageable to the managerial or – better – into a guesthood that takes up its own hospitality.

Not to read divine omnipotence as desiring and devising this situation is to cancel the Qurʾan's doctrine of creation and its perception of creaturehood in this obvious vocation to be 'in and at the world' as veritable stake-holders under Allah's sure mandate. It is also to call in question the whole enterprise identified by Muhammad's sending as 'the Apostle of God'. A world without entrusted humans would mean a world without need of such 'presences' as 'the goodly fellowship of prophets'. Only as *khulafaʾ* are we subjects for their ministry. All that is divinely due *to* us *from* them of directive and guidance relates to what is entrusted *in* us. In caring for our frailty their mission underwrites our dignity.

It follows that we need an understanding of the omnipotence of God consistent with the whole enterprise of creation and with long prophetic mission ministering to its significance as a venture with humankind not – as the angels feared – 'the mistake of creation'[29] but as the very fabric of its drama.

There remains one final consideration about human experience in creaturehood as we have traced it. The *khaliqah* in the *khilafah* – the creature in the 'dominion' – does it extend to any inner liability for the structure of the faith by which it understands itself? We have seen how the intelligent explores the intelligible and, only so, implements the given *magisterium* by which, in society and economy, in culture and sciences, humankind fulfills humanity. We take the mandate to become what we are. The 'given' has to be the achieved. There is an onus to take up, as we have argued earlier. It is an onus we are qualified to bear and the world affords it an answering arena. That *laʿalla* is everywhere at stake. 'Perhaps you will . . .' and all the arts, the sciences, the deeds, the realisations are waiting their release. Such is our 'dominion' in the yielding world.

But does what is thus vested in our active trust cover, or include, the

12

faith by which, in the *taqwa* sense, we are 'religious'? Can we assume any legitimate responsibility for the convictions by which it is discerned? Does that 'Perhaps you may . . .' apply only to the exploits, or can it reach into the absolutes, of life? Can our *khilafah* – that liability to fulfill our self-hood – extend to what defines it, namely religion?

Jews, Christians and Muslims, if not the Bible and the Qur'an, answer differently. It is, however, noteworthy that the Qur'an pleads for something like our inquisition of things to be applied to its own contents. 'Do they not reflect on the Qur'an,' asks Surah 47.24 'or are hearts under lock?' Surah 4.82 repeats the query, clearly implying that if only they did so its integrity would be clear enough. Crudely, it invites inspection, one might say. What such query/enquiry might embrace will always be elastic, encompassed by due reservation. For elsewhere it makes quite uncompromising demands on unquestioning attention. Yet at least the appeal to due cognisance, right interrogation, of what one hears or reads is there. Revealed Scriptures are not for the thoughtless or those content with mere citation. The Biblical: 'Let us reason together . . .' or 'Your reasonable worship . . .' have their place. The inquisitions we were required, by the nature of things, to make into the world at large in order to be authentically the human selves we are, may perhaps also be our duty in fully possessing our faith also. Perhaps not. We have to remit the question to later chapters. Meanwhile, it is the very prelude to the next chapter.

Chapter 2

Engaging Human Means to Divine Ends – The Mission of Messengers

---

I

W<small>ITH CREATION MAKING FOR A HUMANLY</small> legible cosmos according to the Semitic mind, we have no cause to doubt 'a certain sympathy' of either of their Scriptures for the other. The 'letting be' studied in the previous chapter of things cosmic and things human has ensured a Biblical/Quranic world of comparably 'serious' meaning. The nothingness has been taken away – if we may express the concept of creation in that way. Neither has to say with old Thomas Hardy, commenting on 'the blank non-purposiveness of the universe':

> Altogether the world is such a bungled institution from a humane point of view that a grief more or less hardly counts.[1]

Is it not that very 'humane point of view' that registers its protest – a protest that has meaning only because it wills to read a verdict which would answer it? Like the Muslim *Shahadah*, what it needs to repudiate can sanely be only in the name of the affirmation where it has its vindication. The need to deny, in either case, has its ground only in the warrant to assert. Semitic faiths are committed to the significance of the being of our humanness in where, and how, and as we are, in the given trust of this terrestrial scene. If that confidence of theirs is vain or vacuous we are somehow – and impossibly – returning to the nothingness as if, in the given-ness of things, it had never been taken away. Thus faith in the created order, interpreted in humankind as a suited realm, is simply to accept our 'being here and being such' and to do so as receiving and saluting it with all that our response can comprehend. It means a will to be because being is. Such are 'dominion' and *khilafah*.

At once here there is a reproach we must take out of the equation. It is that this humano-centric view of things is quite inordinately arrogant. It should take better, humbler stock of the vast immensities of the universe and the incomprehensible measures of time and admit the utter insignificance to which they assign us in our fleeting, negligible tenure of historical time. The so-called anthropic principle we plead is vanity, all vanity.

This argument asks to be turned on its head. Significance can only be had where it is cognized. We should not be 'vulgarized' by immensities that do not know themselves as such until we tell them. The very 'we are here-ness' alone informs them. The vastnesses that dwarf the human mind signify only in the minds they dwarf. What they might 'mean' otherwise they cannot say. If there be existences like our own somewhere in those infinite spaces our conscious nexus with them will be our achieving. Nor will their being invalidate our own. Our working Semitic sense of our 'being-here-ness' will digest the knowledge.

Whatever may yet eventuate in the knowledge and exploration of space we have only contrived by being radically terrestrial and the radically terrestrial has been the resourcefully human. The Semitic sense of 'possessing possession-earth' has been vindicated, however far the long history has departed from the other part of the Semitic rubric that held us liable to God. Now the very achievements of our possessing competence have arrived where they jeopardise the vital equilibrium of planetary resources and the very globe's integrity. The whole concept of *khilafah*, given and taken, warranted only as a trust, if pursued as a perquisite, threatens in the contemporary world to forfeit itself in a story of subversive sabotage. 'A serious time on serious earth', indeed.

II

Having explored all that must lie between the two clauses of Islam's *Shahadah* – this divine assigning of the fulfilling care of the created order into a human creaturehood designed to accomplish the divine intention for it – how is the creaturely to be 'discipled' into the task?

The Semitic answer, Biblical and Quranic alike, has always been 'By words' – words that will perpetuate in 'writings', words that are understood, in Islam's case, to be eternally inscribed, a pre-existent text given to be humanly uttered until it is again a Book on earth, to be in turn perpetually recited down the generations, their times possessing its eternity.

The Hebraic and the Christian in their different ways are likewise, in turn, 'the people of the Book', of the 'Book' that is theirs in a God-given-ness qualifying them to be its 'people'. 'According to the Scriptures' is their abiding formula, *Kata tas graphas, secundum Scriptores* their sure rubric.

The human scene will be regulated by words, divine words: the creaturely order tutored by language. 'Dominion'/*khilafah* will be educated into its dignity and duty by speech. 'God spake these words and said . . .' announces the Ten Commandments. The directive *fa qul*, 'Say . . .' is the bidding to Muhammad that occurs in the Qur'an more than three hundred times.[2] 'Remember the words of the Lord Jesus how He said . . .', Paul characteristically notes in addressing the Ephesian elders (Acts 20:35). It was that sure instinct which accounted for the steady emergence of the Gospels to be the recorded theme of the formative Christian event, and – as such – rehearsed for evermore.

Thus 'Words' eternalised in 'scriptures' are the hallmark of Semitic religions. They bind in one the faith in creation and the crux of creaturehood. 'By the word of the Lord were the heavens made', cries the psalmist (33:6), to be echoed by the Fourth Evangelist: 'In the beginning was the Word' (1:1) – the initiative of utterance that allows him to sense the continuity with the initiative in Christ whose whole significance, likewise, can be comprehended as 'that which we have heard' and so also 'seen and handled of the word of life' (First Epistle of John 1:1–3).

This unmistakable centrality of 'language' in the Semitic world has often led Hindus, for example, to comment on a 'very talkative religion', maybe because their Hinduism lacked 'the serious earth' which is the corollary of 'the nothingness taken away' by creation. In any event words are irreplaceable. We need them even for the praise of silence. 'Faith comes by hearing and hearing by the word.' 'Who has believed our report?' is always the situation, in that credence and incredulity alike turn on the 'address system' language affords.

We humans cannot escape or elude this necessity of language in its very co-existence with thought, making a sort of *poesis*, or 'inter-texture', to afford in language a ministry of metaphor to meaning whereby, as Wordsworth had it, the Infinite Being accommodates Himself to finite capacity – a capacity lodged in perception of phenomena leading via the senses to concepts words alone will trade.[3] It is part of the very logic of creation for creaturehood that words should be the telling of the realisation of the one in the other, as cognizable, articulate and thereby transactable in will and deed, in art and science, in culture and community.

Hence, in the long Semitic tradition, 'message' in its errand to 'trustees', the 'missive' in the care of some 'apostle' sent to bring it. Hence again the 'scripturality' of the 'verbalism'. In Bible and Qur'an alike, prophethood is the verbal education of entrusted creaturehood, the supreme tribute to its dignity, the crucial factor in its performance.[4] The Hebrew Bible, however, differs radically from the Qur'an in its vital idiosyncrasy as the Scripture of 'the chosen people'. The Qur'an has, to be sure, a crucial Arabism from its very *mise-en-scène* but in no way in any Hebraic sense – an exceptionality for which it has only deep reproach.

Even so, there is a discernible 'sympathy' in the two situations confronting the 'messengerships' addressing and admonishing their respective societies, despite the evident contrasts. That of the Bible scene as far back as Elijah centers – for our purposes – on the supremely ethical 'writing'[5] prophets from Amos to Malachi and comprehends centuries of 'entrusted words' whose burdens chime with grim historical events under the threat, and the reality, of great heathen powers. The whole is poised to interpret the moral meaning of this loaded history and the ultimate forfeiture it brings to both the northern and the Judean kingdoms.

By contrast, the apostolate of Muhammad is to a single city community, economically precarious, no doubt, but secure enough in its pagan worships. It is a thoroughly local mission, despite echoes in the Qur'an of a wider world whether down in the Yemen or northward where Greek and Persian contend remotely. Yet, for all these and other disparities, both Scriptures are set for the assertion of a single unitary theism against all alternative trust, naming or worship. That decisive urge in Muhammad's cry that 'only Allah is God' may seem in the Bible's world to have been axiomatic about Yahweh from the outset, as somehow rooted in the whole concept of 'covenant' and the saga of land-entry and possession. Hebrews were no Quraish on every count of identity and story.

Yet a more careful view – and much modern scholarship – have reason to scrutinise that assured monotheism as explicit even from Abraham. Was it not rather a long and often unsure development until the Deuteronomist and the Isaiahs, one oscillating with an intermittent mono-latry?[6] That query has to negotiate with how the traditional view takes its Bible. Hosea, for example, reads: 'I have been Yahweh your God ever since the land of Egypt, you know no God but Me and beside Me there is no saviour' (13:5). 'Know', however, can be an ambiguous word and there is evidence enough that the exclusivity of His worship meant constant struggle for its ideal purity both of soul and ritual. Israel needed its Elijah because there were those infamous 'prophets of Baal'. It had its Ahab with his Jezebel. Hosea himself had to turn the tables on baal-worship by deftly bringing the popular, rustic sense of 'husbandry' into the sure province of the single Lord who alone gave them 'the corn and wine and oil'.[7] Land-love was not false or obscene: it was only misdirected when 'married' with those plural baals.

Had not the Decalogue itself warned: 'You shall *have* no gods but Me,' clearly conceding – by the verb itself – that, the plural possibility being present, needed to be forbidden? What was the 'monotheism' that still wanted to say: 'He is *a* great king above all gods' (Psalm 95:3) if indeed He was God alone? As against emotional, or maybe circumstantial pluralism,[8] the exclusive reality of God alone, a monotheism that possesses an entire psyche, individual or corporate – these are not blithely held and kept against the grain of human fears or surmises or devices.

The evident presence of this scenario in the whole Biblical world is just the actuality which, despite all disparities, coincides with the thrust of Muhammad's mission. If we will allow the great contrasts in the *mise-en-scène* and let either, as it were, speak with the other, the onus of prophetic words is, indeed, 'Let God be God,' 'Let Yahweh be the One Lord He is,' '*Allahu akbar*, none like unto Him.' What is kindred here is in no way a theological identity between Yahweh and Allah, seeing that predicates denoting them are crucially other. It belongs only in the single mandate of either 'mission' and of each Scripture as we now possess them, to make good divine unity by their verbal travail and their sustained insistence.

Issues in Biblical exegesis here concerning puzzlement about how and when the crowning themes of Exodus, land and 'chosen people' conviction took hold can be postponed to Chapter 6 on 'the writ of readers'. However scholars, querulous or otherwise, choose to resolve them will not affect the basic theme of how a monotheism striving to make itself effectively definitive in soul and society dominates all else that contrasts the Hebraic with the Meccan. The former had their *mushrikun* in the compromises of the renegades, the traitors against whom the likes of Amos had to cry and with whom the pathos of Hosea had to plead.

The Qur'an in the Meccan scene lacks the panoramic 'theatre' set by Chaldean and Assyrian power and the sense of a given destiny that gave rise to Messianic hope. No threat of exile loomed over the Quraish, and the Qur'an drew the lessons of history only from broken ruins and the memory of departed tribes. Yet Muhammad no less than Biblical spokesmen invokes the evidences of rain and storm, of well and date-grove, of seasons and landscapes in their cycles, to disavow all pagan distortion of these energies of nature as tokens of demonic forces and rescue them for the patent truth of the One 'beneficent Lord'. On this theme – though not on historic dispensations – the psalmody of the Qur'an approximates closely to 'sweet singers of Israel.'

That, in such measure, a comparability between them belongs – and belongs significantly[9] – is further argued from the fact that Muhammad's situation, for all its urgent quality of single-handed confrontation, did not altogether want for monotheistic precedent. Something of the ambivalence that attaches to the finalising of Hebrew monotheism has to be allowed in respect of the Quranic status and story of those *hunafa'*, the Arab theists of the Qur'an.[10] They needed to be distinguished from 'Jews and Christians' and they claimed their own kinship with Abraham. Formative as their influence may have been in Muhammad's own *Sirah*, it in no way counter-parted in the Arabian context the defining theism of the Hebraic tradition feeding on the destiny of Exodus and the territorial mind-set central to their theology. So much is clear from the very arduousness of Muhammad's own mission in face of an obduracy and a

18

bitterness untouched by any Hanafi presence or legend. Whatever their legacy may have been, the unremitting task was his alone.

Moreover, the Prophet of the Qur'an was so distantly lonely in the sequence of Semitic prophethood to which he appealed. It had been silent in Judeo-Israel for several centuries and he was far removed in time from those messengers to the tribes of ʿAd and Thamud. The Hebrew prophets of their final centuries were mostly near contemporaries. Biblical and Quranic situations have their irreconcilable contrasts. None the less the prophetic mind is that the call to 'have no other gods', to 'let God alone be God', is a vocation relentless in its claim on tenacity and endurance. Plural worships in every context are tenacious of their own delusions, slow to heed what would dissuade and subdue them, and defiant against surrender.

III

It follows that, however minimal we are minded to count it, there *is* this real 'sympathy' between Bible and Qur'an in the 'policy' of words, and in the arduous 'burden' of their task. If, as steadily appears in both Scriptures, the verbal task is found to be daunting and unrelenting, apprehensive of its own failure, what can mere language come by to fortify its cause?

One immediate factor, doubtless, is its own status as 'divinely given'. 'These are the very words of Yahweh.' 'He revealed to His servant what He revealed.' If, as ever the case, there is scepticism on this count, the word-bringer can only fall back on vindication by content. For the basic reality of prophethood is not primarily about 'forecasting' futures but about honest summons to present realism, with the future only and for ever turning on the answer. In the case of the Qur'an the supreme 'here-and-now' demand about the ultimate *Yaqin* – that impending 'last assize' – could never come into demonstration like the Fall of the Northern Kingdom or the actuality of exile, to which Hebrew prophets appealed.[11] Of 'forecasting' in history there is little in the Qur'an, whereas it looms large and vivid in the Biblical scene, the latter being so far a uniquely historicized world.[12]

The Qur'an's word-mission is sustained by appeal to the far past attested by the ruins, at Mada'in Salih and else where, if discerned there are manifest tokens of the nemesis on unbelief. For the tribes, long extinct by these evidences, had been obdurate against their messengers. These belonged with the archaeology of revelation, fit to corroborate the spoken message by visual imagination. Hebraic prophethood, by contrast, was intensely pre-occupied with the immediate political situation and its open menace alike to land and people. Its patently legible 'ruins' could well be those of its own bastions and walls, its besieged palaces and 'ivory towers', the prey of all too brutal present enemies.

Word-bearing, in either case, was also fortified by the sense of standing in a long tradition. That 'vineyard' parable to which we must return of 'sendings' in a long succession characterises those vital centuries between Amos and Malachi.[13] In different idiom an even longer fraternity of spokesmen marks the Qur'an's sense of 'books' (even 'sheets') and scriptures, so that Muhammad was strengthened by their precedent, under the pressure of maligning 'non-hearers'. It has always been central to the Qur'an's doctrine of itself that it was 'confirming' all previous sacred texts and bringing their identical message. However tense in its controversies or tangled in its evidences, there is no doubt that the Qur'an claims to resume a commonalty of 'word missions' from God whereby human 'agencies' pass from action into 'divine literature', from eternal realms into human legibility by lip and eye and mind. In that sense Quranic *tajwid* or 'recitation' and its calligraphy are in a disparate tradition that is nevertheless congenial with the Biblical scene.

Stimulus to 'word-bringers' as a hallowed succession was, it might have seemed, disheartening insofar as the constant need of repetition might argue the futility of them all. That heavy burden, if and when it was registered, belongs here elsewhere in the argument. What could have banished that suspicion in the case of Muhammad – though the adversities were many – may have arisen from the distinctive assurance of the Qur'an that its 'voice' in Mecca and Medina would duly bring the long succession to an end. Prophethood would have its last words and find its ultimate 'seal' in his own *Sirah*, as the last, irrepeatable culmination of them all. The 'perfecting of religion' (Surah 5.3, cf. 3.19) in *Al-Islam* meant that all duly 'holy writ' had come to final terms with time.

It remains puzzling to know from where this ruling conviction came, inasmuch as sequence and succession had from the outset been defining features of all such guiding, admonishing 'revelation'. As Islam itself learned so soon, there was no ground for assuming that humankind had become finally and permanently heedful. The assurance could only have been that, the last words having been said, the inclusive truth written, human society had no further need of their mediation. The divine 'enough' had been sent: the human amenability would follow, as it were, *ipso facto*. Perhaps that Islamic reliance on 'effectual word' has to be explained by the sharp absence of any Messianic dimension of the Biblical order in the Quranic world.[14]

Is it relevant to ask whether Malachi – only 'named' by his office – perceived or knew himself as the last member of the 'goodly fellowship'? We do not know. Mysteriously, Hebraic prophethood gave way to Wisdom literature and the Greek influence. There was an unaccountable lapse from the genius of the Isaiahs and the anguish of Jeremiah. How did it transpire that something believing itself akin should have appeared a millennium later in the bare soil of Arabia? It had been the assumption in the Hebraic tradition that Yahweh's 'messengers' were only recruited from and commissioned to Yahweh's people. Prophethood was a hallmark of Jewry alone, given the land, the history and the identity to which it alone belonged. That sense of things, if still persisting in their late Arabian diaspora, was ground enough for their non-recognition of Muhammad.

Yet that 'people' have their 'prophets' in their own 'language', to yield them 'books' which make them a cohesive and highly self-conscious people – all this was discernible enough to Muhammad from the Jewish tradition he encountered. Could these several items – books deriving from prophets, prophets having books and both cementing identities – have been the impetus to Muhammad's sense of mission, his recourse to Mount Hira’ in meditation, his alertness to the *hunafa’*, and his conviction as a 'sent-one', this Arab *Rasul-Allah*? The grounds of an attainment of authenticity, first inward and then – agonisingly – outward are always mysterious. Islam in history is witness that it was so: the Qur’an of faith and the faith of the Qur’an eventuated. There can be no doubt that precedents Biblical were formative and that, at length, the strength they had sponsored in origins passed into one perpetuated into contradiction. Verbalism on the divine part was the heavenly policy in engaging human means to divine ends. So all Semitic Scriptures testify. Arabic might belong with prophethood no less than Hebrew and come to do so by precedents it would both emulate and alienate.

IV

That the Qur’an was 'luminous Arabic' was central to Muhammad's self-assurances among the several other factors so far noted. 'We have sent it down an Arabic Qur’an' is the frequent insistence of the text about itself.[15] If the divine mind was employing exclusively the verbal method of encompassing divine ends from human means, in that locale, it was proof-bearing to do so in the native tongue.

Moreover this matchlessness (*I‘jaz*) of the Qur’an as Arabic was a telling factor on several counts. It fulfilled the long tradition that 'prophets' were 'to their own country'. There was assumed nexus between preacher and hearers in every case and 'no people to whom a prophet was not sent'. Tribal familiars belonged with tribal pleas and warnings. Further the powerful poetic excellence of the Qur’an, in disclaiming mere verbal skills, yet resembled and excelled them in appeal to the long cherished esteem of them in the Meccan scene. Thus Muhammad roundly denied that the deliverances from his lips were no more than the feats of verse, assonance

21

and rhythm his people eagerly savoured and which their language so amply afforded. Their content anyway would more than disabuse the popular mind of such conclusions. Yet he could still challenge them to 'produce a surah (even ten surahs) comparable' to his eloquence. He could vindicate his authenticity on the very human grounds he must also disown, in that only *wahy* (or heavenly diction) had bestowed the marvel on him.[16]

Herein was a fascinating integration of the divine and the human. The Qur'an's poetry might, for attestation's sake, associate itself, by challenge to emulate or excel, issued to an intrigued audience, with their most esteemed Arabic pride, yet – in that very gesture – assert its total non-human order as of unique divine disclosure. Arabic, as the earthly context most prized it, could carry – indeed constitute – the eternal Scripture on the 'preserved tablet' (85.22) nevertheless with credentials a particular terrestrial literary culture could identify and appreciate by its own norms, at once employed and left behind.[17]

This sense of the Qur'an's inherent revelatory thrust seems confirmed by the continuing Islamic doctrine of its inalienable Arabicity, the fact that it is 'untranslateable'. This dogma has to be overridden in practice and in some circles is foregone altogether. If contents are to be inclusively intelligible they must be capable of rendition in any and every language. Indeed such intelligibility (in the immediate time and place of Mecca) is simply for the purpose of 'warning *umm al-Qura*' (i.e. Mecca, 42.7) By that rubric translation becomes mandatory, just as any 'incarnation', or – here – 'inverbalization' has to be intelligible within any and every culture, though necessarily first incident for only one.

Much else lies behind this *I'jaz*, this 'inimitability' of the Qur'an, but our interest here is in its force as a powerful corollary of the verbal shape of the divine will for human means by response from our *khilafah*. The challenge to 'imitate' the Qur'an was not taken up in terms that might ever have competed and, in any event, Muhammad was insistent to disavow any resemblance to the skills needed. Emulation, though invited, was beyond attainment by virtue of its divine origin. Yet language, via its quality vetted by the immediate culture, grammar and poetic art, was made inseparable from its religious message.[18]

V

Given this entire reliance on language in Islamic – though not in Biblical Scriptures[19] – the question must follow: how amenable, how persuadable, is the human condition? We remember Isaiah's: 'The ox knows his owner and the ass his master's crib, but Israel does not know, My people do not consider' (1.3). Does Micah call on 'the mountains to hear the

Lord's controversy' (6.2) because people are inattentive? How insistently do the Hebrew prophets re-iterate their cry: 'Hear ye the word of the Lord'?

The Quranic scene is similar and we need to ponder it more closely, mindful of how different its close focus and its initial audience of *jahiliyyah*. 'Hear . . . the controversy' might almost be the clue we need. For Muhammad's 'hearers' were for thirteen harsh years stubbornly non-hearers, so much so that their long obduracy is taken up into the very texture of the Book, through his summons to 'Say' so far required by their 'counter-saying'. That situation would seem to have five clear characteristics, reaches of non-hearing on five sharp counts. They inter-act.

That the Qurʾan was Arabic, with the implications just studied, related to the suspicion of the heedless that it was alien. Surah 16.103 notes the charge that 'he had it from a stranger' while 41.44 derides the idea that 'this Qurʾan' would ever have been in 'an alien speech'. How could it be when he, Muhammad, was 'an Arab' and (53.2) their 'kinsman' and (90.2) 'citizen of this city'. Surah 26.198 insists how incompatible the Qurʾan would have been with any other – and strange – folk. It was in and as the vernacular.

But, secondly, if not alien it was subversive. The Quraish of Mecca saw Muhammad's mission as counter to their vested interests as presiding over a plural shrine with its lucrative pilgrimage and vital status, as well as a precarious commerce.[20] As such it also subverted the traditions of their heritage and threatened to be disruptive of all they held dear, the code of honour and of revenge.

Moreover, thirdly, it was eminently refutable by their lights – this isolation in unity of the Allah they already named as supreme over a multiplicity of lesser beings whom their anxieties, fears and daily experiences needed to mediate the incidence of wells and storms, of rains and droughts, of births and deaths. And what of this foolish doctrine Muhammad had about bones and sinews coming together in a 'resurrection' to face some final scrutiny of all life's gathered deeds? Their poetry of mortal pathos made nonsense of such notions of survival with such dire – or blissful – exaggerations of what human frailty had in store for it, when the reality was the misery of burial into silence.

Fourthly, if we read aright the Qurʾan's tally of what heeded only to disparage, what was alien, subversive, refutable, was by every such token pretentious or self-contrived. Muhammad, being on these counts socially unwanted, was also personally abnormal, with those withdrawals to his cave of *Tahannuth*[21] and his, to them, inordinate sense of 'mission'. 'Your kinsman is not misled' (53.2) they needed to be assured. It was this fusion of all their Quraishi obloquy into personal calumny that surely occasioned the vindication the Qurʾan affords him – in his own right and task – such as 68.4; 'Truly you are of a noble order',[22] or 94.4: 'We have exalted your reputation', as well as several allusions to 'lightening his burden' or attesting his vocation.

It is here that a striking – if potential – feature of 'sympathy' between Scriptures becomes evident, namely how the person of the 'messenger' is inevitably fused into the import of the 'message'. While Islam possesses the Qur'an strictly as divine words in which Muhammad plays no personal part, except as their recipient and mouthpiece, it does read his persona as that of 'the ideal Muslim', from whose character and behavioural precedents stored in Tradition, elements of *Shari'ah* are duly and extensively drawn. This 'truth through personality' would seem to be at least latent, if never explicit, in respect of the Qur'an itself. As we have noted, contention around what he 'said' could not but extend into controversy about who he 'was'. The writ of the one hinged on the status of the other. What *risalah* is this? incredulity asked. It was a question that had to pass into What *rasul* is this? The two were manifestly inseparable, the credibility of either fused into the other.

It was emphatically this way also in Hebraic prophethood. The impact of the herdsman, Amos, on the 'ivory palaces' of Samaria was at least as much in who he was as in what he said. Indeed, his deriders concentrated their unheeding in their disdain for his person and his origins, saying: 'Go home where you belong with your sycamores in Tekoa.' Likewise he could only respond by identifying his persona as no professional seer but one whom the Lord had sent (Amos 7:12–15). With Hosea, intimate events from his own personal life suggest the very core of his message about the 'apostasy' of his people under the analogy of marital betrayal. Why should Jeremiah have been so sure of a destiny from the womb, if the entire personality was not the seed-bed and wine-press of all that he survived to say?[23] It is evident enough from this measure of 'word-in-self' why New Testament faith should have learned to identify a 'oneness of messenger and message' in its perception of 'the Word made flesh'.

There, doubtless, Islam would lay its veto and the thoughts involved are pointing forward where we are not ready to come. At this point in 'sympathetic' study we can only say that the Qur'an turns, not only exclusively but contextually, on the ever crucial presence of Muhammad immersed in a human situation within which alone the deliverances that are 'the Book' move and have their being. The very fact that doctrine precludes his conscious participation in its contents only makes that presence the more significant. Have not *asbab al-nuzul*, 'the occasions of the sending down', in time, place and context, always been crucial to exegesis and comprehension, linking 'what' with 'where' and 'when?' Occasions only happen inside biography.

VI

The foregoing points to a haunting question about 'the way of words' as engaging human means to divine ends. Does it avail? Can it succeed? The issue awaits the ensuing chapter and some careful study of the adverse experience of messengers emerging from the chapter we leave. What should we conclude from the long prophetic sequence in lineal succession? How should we interpret the strange demise of prophethood in Israel? Is there something about human nature that finds admonishment tedious, develops a resistance to what advertises its wrongs, turns aside from messengers, and is dissuaded by persuaders? If there is truly an autonomy granted as *khilafah*, why should *khilafah* spell an obligation which – we might suspect – leaves us no longer autonomous? Is our sense, taught as the essence of Semitic creaturehood, of having genuine tenancy and tenure here, somehow also some 'negative indicative' messengers are set to have us understand? On all these counts, could it be that law itself, its commands and prohibitions, kindle – out of our very autonomy – a will to counter them?

The questions ramify and bewilder. Yet it is our given *khilafah* that wants to ask them on the very way to learning that the mastery it bestowed was truly meant for a right quality of 'submission'. The long and arduous task of prophethood lay in having us understand, beyond all rebellion and contradiction, the true authority in surrender, the liberty in law's genuine privilege.

That crisis was the very name of 'messenger' experience.

Chapter 3

The Crisis in Messenger Experience

I

WHY THE EVER UNCOMPULSIVE WORD proves always less than compelling in the human world is the constant perplexity of honest religion or, indeed, hardly compelling at all. That humanity disappoints the idealist is evident enough to the secular mind, but faiths Semitic, believing in the divine mandate for righteous submission, are still more at loss about the inconclusive results in the long frustrations of human history and in the too sorry spectacle of their own story. Doubtless they may silence any mind for due misgivings by strident re-assertion of themselves, by recourse to an absolutism of claim and rule, ignoring the ultimate religious temper by way of forfeit to a pretentious arrogance.

Words are all that 'messengers' have and words, by their nature, cannot well ride roughshod over hearts and minds and wills. For it is these they address, these they are set to recruit and recruit into assent is their whole intention – an intention which requires them to rely only on themselves. The verbal, as verbal, attains and avails only through consent. It has no other sanction, brings no other warrant, than its own search for what will heed it. That its reliance is exclusively upon its content is precisely why it is so well employed in the address – as Semitic faiths have it – to human *khilafah* and 'dominion'. For these are ours in their character as volitional and privileged, liable for direction only in that they are capable of attention – and both 'by hearing of the word'. That word and words should be the means employed is the divine tribute to our dignity, the dignity divinely given and not somehow compromised in the way by which its obligations seek for it.

Our reflection on 'language' and God's use of it may seem too obvious for exposition, if only the point, as the 'divine policy of language', was not so far forgotten. Words, especially those of command, are indeed meant to be performative. They are only so in being heeded. Where there is recourse to enforcement words are superseded. Language then concedes its own failure.

The 'messenger' role in its verbal vocation shares this experience of latent hazard in its whole reliance upon response. Its theme and mission may be mandatory in content but that quality, merely by being such, does not translate into auditory acceptance and result. Messenger fidelity may well cause its import to 'carry' and prophethood is not betrayed. Yet, meeting heedlessness and unconcern, its very 'arriving' is denied its errand and prophethood is left forlorn.[1] Language – sacred language most of all – is at the mercy of its means. It is hostage in the listeners' world.

It follows that missions bound over to language are liable to keen anxiety and implicit suffering. They do not merely become the focus of indifference, they may well excite a hostility to which initial indifference leads and will lead the more, the more language urges what it has at heart in face of thwarted ends.

II

That this situation in the experience of messengers looms large alike in the Bible and the Qur'an, is evident enough. Even the redoubtable Elijah, for all his resources of strategy beyond his verbal eloquence, or perhaps because of them, found himself disconsolate and defeated in spirit under 'a juniper tree'. More significantly, the Isaiahs, Micahs, Zechariahs and Hoseas of the Hebrew Bible were all to varying degrees the butt of scorn and the target of enmity. Their times, to be sure, were vexed by political dooms and alien invasions, with threats to their beloved people, but these were only the more dire by personal isolation and popular contempt. In several cases, as most notably with Hosea, these factors entered significantly into the very substance of their witness. So far was this so that it was fitting to say of Jeremiah:

> Prophecy had already taught its truths, its last effort was to reveal itself in a life.[2]

He had said: 'I sat alone because of Thy hand' (15:17) weighing the bitter loneliness his words entailed upon him – loneliness and worse through the perils of siege, prison and exile. Given the historical setting of those generations from Amos to Malachi it would have been impossible to 'bring divine words' without sharp personal yearning and 'inward pain'. To be 'revealed in a life' was for each and all the final destiny of being called to preach. To be no more than 'the voice of one crying' (Isaiah 40:3) was, inwardly as well as outwardly, 'a wilderness vocation'. What is notable about this Biblical 'travail of the soul' with these 'prophets of the word' is that none of them (we are long after Elijah) resorted to violence in the interests of their word. They entered and harangued the courts of kingship and preached in the corridors of power but they never took these into partnership. They were not minded to implement their meanings by any cult of force or physical threatening or made themselves parties to the incidence of what, of requital, they feared for their hearers. Their commitment to the verbal was absolute. For it was there even in the acted symbolisms the likes of Ezekiel devised, the 'signs' by which he brought home his meanings, naïve as they sometimes seem and almost bizarre. Resort to them was only part of a total commitment to the spoken theme. Words could even notably serve them in the very names Hosea and Isaiah bestowed on their offspring, to ensure that the message would outlive their generation.

So far were they from 'force-wielders' that Hosea, for example, was ready to foresee times when 'Israel would long abide without king and prince' and still return to 'seeking the Lord' (3:4). Given their dire warnings about historic retribution, they could incur the very charge of treachery against the state in the passion of their words. Micah, in this context, takes the 'might' word used in the Books of Kings and Chronicles to denote their prowess and identifies it with the trenchancy of his preaching words (3:8). The contrasting nature of the 'power' in words could not be more complete. Zechariah's formula: 'Not by might nor by power but by My spirit . . .' (4:6) was the rubric of Hebrew prophethood. They laid plumblines down fortress walls (Amos 7:7–8, Zechariah 4:10) but their only siege-hammer was their eloquence.

This near fusion of word and personality in the Hebraic scene or, rather, of personality as word, is discernible in the music and imagery of their language. Their telling parallelism is familiar even in translation: 'The grass withers, the flower fades': 'arise, shine, for thy light is come, the glory of the Lord is risen upon you.' Their imagination feeds on the landscape they cherish. There is Hosea with his 'corn and wine and oil' as in a chorale of celebration, while Habakkuk invokes 'the fig-tree, the olive, the field and the flock' as the divine fidelities that measure the 'nevertheless' of his determination to be gladly confident in his Lord even were they to fail (3:17–18).

Or there is rustic Amos taking his metaphor from the Tekoan landscape – the roar of the lion, the viper lurking in the crevices of a wall, or the decaying carcass of fallen prey. With such vivid imagery to hand he has little need to reach for the inventive analogies that are not beyond his wit, while he is competent to draw on sundry historic precedents to illumine his message.

Most abiding of all, in the Isaiahs and elsewhere, there are the 'bucolics' of shepherd and sheep, establishing the pastoral image at the very heart of Biblical theology and, later, at the core of New Testament ministry. While 'the people of His pasture and the sheep of His hand' was an originally 'privatizing' theme its appeal – despite climatic, territorial diversity – gave it a universal purchase on the yearning soul of faith.

In its own time and place there is a comparable harmony of text and landscape in the Qur'an and its doxologies. There also the summons from prophethood is sustained by the same celebration of the natural order as the sphere of divine reality and the legible concert of 'signs' that 'sacramentalise' the experience of the Arab camp, of cameleer and citizen, of oases and their environs of shade and refuge. Even the sails of dhows on the Red Sea and the winds they harness are evidence of Allah's bounty.[3] If Muhammad was 'declared free of this land', the multiple possible meanings told how alert his speech in the Qur'an would be, replete with its tangible yield of metaphor and parable – the sudden rains, the deceptive contours of shifting sands, the dried-up well, the illusion of hope born of the cheating mirage. All these, if Quranic loyalty will allow us to think so, argue 'a certain sympathy' with the Biblical world in respect of how prophethood reinforces its word by virtue of the natural order and how, doing so, personality possesses language.

III

That 'sympathy' extends beyond these obvious aspects of the two Scriptures. It belongs also with the degree to which at least the first thirteen years of Muhammad's *Sirah* with the Qur'an knew the same reality of popular resistance and often scornful heedlessness. In a rare moment where the reader can readily visualise Muhammad with an audience we sense how scant attention might be, even if not dismissive. Having enjoined them to 'remember God frequently that prosperity may be yours' the passage goes on:

> When they have seen a chance of trading or amusement they have gone after it and left you standing there.

Did what follows then avail: 'Say, "The things of God are better"'? or the pointed reminder: 'God is the best of all suppliers of our need'?[4] Trade was a life-line of the Meccans and love of barter abounded. A 'messenger' deemed an upstart had a hard 'problem of communication', the more so when his message came to seem a clear threat to their livelihood.

From all sides it is clear that Muhammad steadily headed into strenuous situations where, in no way minded to remonstrate with Allah like some Arab Jeremiah, he could only endure with *sabr*, that characteristic virtue in the Qur'an, and hold to a patience sustained by renewed re-assurance as to his valid mission. Until near the end of his Meccan years, he had the staunch support of his wife Khadijah and the significant protection of his uncle Abu Talib. These, however, did not reach the inner stresses of calumny and derision only apostolate knows. It was noted earlier how sundry passages sustained him by precedents of the same experience undergone by previous messengers facing a like hostility.

That such stimulus to endurance was crucial in the Meccan situation is evident enough from several references to his register of the evil ranged against him. 'Is it that you are vexing your very soul with grief over the way they are?' asks Surah 18.6, while 76.24 enjoins: 'Await with patience what your Lord determines' adding: 'do not yield to any among them who is an evil-doer or an unbeliever.' The solace at – it would seem – an earlier point came to him in the form of a question:

> Have We not lifted from you the burden that was breaking down your back and have We not established your reputation? (94.3–4)

That 'reputation', where believing credence – though in minority terms – was greeting it in Mecca stood, paradoxically, against the tide of things usual among prophets of the past.

> The Apostle said: 'Lord, my people have been altogether dismissive of this Qur'an.' It has been Our way in the case of every prophet to have him experience enmity from those who are evil bent. (25.30)

The gibes and charges Muhammad underwent had their precedent in an honoured tradition as 51.51–53 observed in terms that certainly reached back to Hebraic times in 'sympathy'.

> Comparably no previous messenger ever came to those in earlier times of whom they did not say: 'he is either a sorcerer or he is mad.' Is this a habit they have passed down to each other?

It was surely these experiences of rejection that evoked his yearning for the assurance only utter confidence in vocation could sustain. Thus the personal dimension of suffering in word-bearing was taken back into the integrity of the word itself. Only the latter could suffice to validate the former, as in 41.41:

> Those who refuse faith in the Reminder (i.e. the Qur'an) when it reaches them – it is nevertheless, a Book of inviolate worth. As a disclosure from on high by One who is all-wise and all-worthy, it is secured against all that is false whether from within or from without.

Thus it was not only that Muhammad's trouble-in-heart merged with the Book's very contents but that the authenticity of either could only belong in that of the other. The reason, in the context of the Book's being Arabic and not alien, is graphically represented in the comment that follows:

As for those who do not believe, it falls, as it were, upon deaf ears or as though it were offered to blind eyes. They are like people being called to from a long way off. (41.44)

For all that is different in ethos, setting and import, it is clear that when the great Hebrew prophets spoke of their 'word-burden' their meaning has some affinity with what the Qur'an tells of something kindred in the Qur'an.[5] 'A certain sympathy' – in textual fact if not in reader recognition – is clear enough.

What, in sequence, is also vital is that this common situation of messenger travail *and* unheeding humans in this inter-action argues the crippling problematics of the 'word-strategy' in persuading human autonomy into ready concurrence with the divine design of *islam*, or 'right-serving', explicit in the gift of it. We have seen that *khilafah* is genuinely given and that prophet-sending is the supreme tribute to its reality. No loyal doctrine of creation, creaturehood and prophethood can hold that 'dominion' as less than genuine, or somehow 'artificial' or illusory, or cancelled by divine omnipotence. For such omnipotence would be indulging in 'jest' and 'toying with us humans' – a folly the Qur'an has explicitly ruled out.

That there was 'risk' in the venture – risk knowingly assumed – is unmistakable in the definitive text of 2.30f. Had the mandate to humans to 'deputise' as the divine means toward the divine ends been phoney, a fraud or a delusion, there would be no relevance in prophethood, nor would we have either the creation or the creaturehood we know and daily occupy as tenanting technicians – and that, now, in the most exacting and awesome measure. The great and grim reality of this autonomy as urgently meant for autonomous surrender into divine intention is fundamental to everything Judaic, Christian and Islamic, not to say also to our sanity.

There is no escape from that conclusion. Why then did messengers travail so to secure it? Why should autonomy consciously withhold from its true destiny? There comes a wondering realisation here that the legitimacy of the human is integral to the nature of the divine.

For there have been versions other than the Semitic about 'creations'. The gnostic notions, like those of the third-century *Corpus Hermeticum*, drawn out of antiquity from the 'wisdom' of Hermes Trimegistus (the triple Magus), taught that it was 'demiurges' who had been involved in the creation of the universe and were gaoled in human bodies in retribution, seeing they had 'rivalled' the gods of creation. Thus it was a sort of retaliatory resentment that made those 'gaoled demiurges' obdurate in their human forms who became braggarts and ne'er-do-wells in an odd scenario.[6] This is a very far cry from the Biblical/Quranic scene, with its generous single Creator and its genuinely human custodians whose fallible frailties have been seen from the outset and painstakingly addressed by messengers in long succession.

Why, then, are they so strangely unpersuadable as to their true dignity, so recalcitrant about their known vocation to a 'service as their freedom'? Why, further, is the divine purpose so patiently uncompulsive? Is it that there is something built into the very nature of 'autonomy' as real that it wants its own unimpeded exercise? Do law and injunction then somehow evoke their own rejection by the very nature of the capacity they call upon? Autonomy must mean that a capacity to obey is also a capacity to withhold obedience. The freedom which is the very principle of *islam*[7] becomes the faculty for non-*islam*?

That certainly seems to be the situation. Hence the element of 'risk' seen as present from the outset. Hence, too, the implicit need to take it in our sort of world – a divine willing to be committed – for moral, not ultimate, purposes – to crucial human cognisance of that order of things.

Clearly the will to say Yes! to the divine way has the will to say No! Otherwise, the Yes! is not of the order of the one required, and required by all that we have studied. The autonomy that can yield to its 'high calling' can descend to its wayward wrong and somehow make all appealing prophethood seemingly futile, except as the ever-present, ever-urgent 'Reminder' and its 'warning'.

IV

It is this crisis inherent in *khilafah* that is captured in the messenger/vine-yard parable which has so marked a place in the New Testament, being found in all three Synoptic Gospels. The retributary aspect it has in the conclusion belongs to the first context of 'chosen peoplehood,' rescued out of Egyptian bondage and planted in the land (Isaiah 5:1–7). But that very particularity symbolises and educates the inclusive human trust with place, time and tribal being. The analogy Jesus uses of 'the absent land-lord' may seem a strange one for never absent, ever-minding Lordship. Two reasons may be discerned behind it. The tradition of such landlords, sending for fruits they had farmed out to tenant-growers, was a common feature of Jesus' Galilee. Indeed, resentments against them fuelled sundry uprisings in the Roman years prior to the great Jewish Revolt of 66–70. Furthermore, the image, strange as it was, indicated that this 'lord in a distant country', while genuinely in charge and possession, had neverthe-less set up a real 'dominion', an over-to-you about the tenancy. It fitted a *khilafah* perfectly. The husbandmen were 'caliphs' in a domain they responsibly farmed.

The issue, right inside such *khilafah*, was how 'responsibly' did they do so? For their tenure contained this paradox, namely that what they had to yield as produce, they could conspire to usurp as their own property. 'Caliphs' were in a position to become owners, precisely because of the 'absence' of the rightful owner – 'absent' in the very form and fashion of their tenure.

This is just what we see happening in the story, via the sequence of the dusty answers to the successive messengers. The Qur'an (2.87) briefly notes the parable in that 'some of them were maligned as liars and some were put to death'. That sequence signals what Christian thought has long recognised as the gravitation of evil downward, the dynamism in the nature of sin. Each refusal of the claim excites – even ensures – a repeat of it at a more dastardly level.[8] From rebuffing the first, they pass to denouncing the second, to beating the third, to slaying the fourth. The sequence proves in vain: mere 'messaging' is found to be futile, except as availing to incriminate the stake-holders. The parable depicts the reach of a non-*islam*, once humans have opted for it and put themselves in fee to their own turpitude.

The point is reached at which they have shown their hand as disowning their *khilafah* by pursuing it as a total autonomy they will exercise in defiance of its true destiny. Whatever the niceties of law and regulation, are they not in physical occupancy? May not such possession become permanent? Surely if they can use the 'absence' to capture the title to the land, they can convert that 'absence' into a legal non-existence.

In the light of these outrages, it seems utter folly for the lord of the vineyard to 'send his son'. Yet is is precisely that sequence of events that demands it. For by their behaviour the tenants are in fact conspiring to take over the ownership. So much is what they have come to mean – and hope – in their acts of repudiation. This being so, only 'the son' will suffice the situation. Only he – as no messenger could – signals and claims the right of the lord. So much the tenants realise in resolving to clinch their plot by killing him. 'This is the heir: let us do away with him and the inheritance will be ours.' The lord has taken the full measure of their insurrection by 'laying on the line' completely what was always at stake in the original 'risk' of planning the *khilafah* which is thus abjured. Autonomy has come full circle in refusing its *islam* by asserting its wilful defiance.

The New Testament parable opens on to a distinctively Christian 'redemption' in this 'sending of the son', to which we must come in its own place.

Meanwhile, the parable remains an arresting commentary on the divine 'verbalism' we have been studying. There *is* this human obduracy which will not abide its admonitions, which disowns the claim and disavows its very writ to summon or to plead.

Given that Islam, in its entirety, turns on this truth of human creaturehood in its *khilafah* as the way of divine ends by human means – and this creaturehood taught and monitored by faithful prophethood – it remains to ask how far the Qurʾan shares this Christian perception of the reach of human wrong? While there are passages that credit sin to frailty of will or mere forgetfulness,[9] and while some in Islam would see our *khilafah* quite over-ridden (and thus cancelled) by God's *qadar* or 'decree', there are emphases that fully engage with what we must call 'the seriousness of sin', the human capacity for radical evil. One of those is the concept of *zulm* and of *zulm al-nafs*. The root and all its derivatives are frequent throughout the Qurʾan. The prime sense of *zulm* is whatever violates the right, the good, the true. Tyranny, extortion, defamation, lying, cheating, killing – all these in the various pursuits of politics, commerce, society and life at large – are the works of *zulm* as gross trespass on another. In two other realms – that of Allah's right to worship and awe – *zulm* is the dire 'wrong' of idolatry. Truly Allah is beyond all 'harm', yet Malachi's ancient question: 'Will a man rob God?' (3.9) could only have from intelligent Muslim the Yes! answer, inasmuch as *Shirk*, false worship, alienates from Allah the worship due to Him alone and directs it, with trust, reliance, hope and fear, where none of these belong. Thus idolatry is heinous wrong.

These social and religious forms of *zulm* constitute what the Qurʾan castigates as *zulm al-nafs*, 'the wronging of the self'. The verdict: 'It was their own selves they wronged' comes almost like a refrain in the Qurʾan's register of unbelief and deeds of evil.[10]

It is arguably close to the mood of Hosea about Israel's forfeiture of its real identity. It surely suggests that when we violate those 'surrendering' terms of our human *khilafah* we disesteem and distort the very autonomy of selfhood which was meant for the divine glory. We violate the given criteria of our creaturehood by a perversity which distorts and degrades its rightful destiny. We have a *nafs*, a soul-in-body being of a self-rebelling order, this being the actuality of the 'dominion' we can rightly, but thus falsely exercise in the evil we opt to do. Or, as the Qurʾan elsewhere reminds us: 'On you are your own souls.'[11]

Thus the centrality of the *zulm-al-nafs* theme in the Qurʾan's understanding of the self, self-violated, comes near to the distinction so crucial in the New Testament between 'wrong' as what I *do* and 'wrong' as how I *am*. By this capacity to disavow the selves we should be – and that by our own decision knowingly made – we pass from the idea of 'sin' as merely the contravention of a rule. It now is seen and known as a state of heart. Thus, again, 'law' itself becomes more than a catalogue of doings to be vetted on a list of regulations: it becomes 'a discerner of the thoughts and intents of the heart'. We can no longer protest: 'I *did* nothing wrong.' Such ready exonerations may only be part of an inner blameworthiness deep in character itself. As the realist Albert Camus often noted in his novels, there is an 'innocence' which is the concealing cloke of guilt.[12] This sense of things is the more urgent, given how far collective vested interests can deprave and override the misgivings of private conscience. For collective passions generate more will to defiance of the good and the right than personal ones, or the latter, in seats of power, subvert private duty to official cause. Thus 'the state', 'establishment', 'the party', 'nationalism', even religion itself – as mosque, or church, or Zion – will embroil their societies in guilt and crime.[13] The perpetrators, then, are no longer in 'the hallowed valley' where mind and soul are aware of 'holy ground' on which they may not trample but where they should 'take off' the shoes of scorn and arrogance.[14]

Zulm al-nafs, inclusive and perverse as it is, is far from the only dimension of the Qur'an's lively awareness of radical wrong. Idolatry (*shirk*) is another and endemic in society, another is *kufr*, the harsh disavowal of messengers and their mission, and telling a gross 'ingratitude' as another of the evils that Scripture often decries. There is that *fasad*, 'corrupting in the earth', which Surah 2.30f had foreseen as likely human behaviour.

What, further, of that *istikbar* in 35.43, that blatant arrogance which, like the husbandmen parable, went back on its own pledge of obedience and

> . . . when a warner came to them the only result was their intensified disgust, their arrogance in the land and evil scheming.

References are many to this habit of overweening pride, of disdain for the appeal of divinely 'sent-ones'. There are no less than thirty occasions when the Qur'an makes devastating comment on what Latin would dub *superbia*, a boastful pride in excess of evil.[15]

Elsewhere this quality of inveterate wrong is characterised as 'those in whose hearts there is a sickness', as in 5.52. and some nine other verses. The imagery is different but there is no disguising the reach of human obduracy in defaulting from all *khilafah* intended for righteous well-being. The Qur'an sees and tells the same pattern of recalcitrance as the Gospel parable. The evident 'sympathy' of both Scriptures meets in this panorama of historic malaise and wilful contrariety.

It may be that instances of *istikbar* and *marad fi-l-Qulub*, 'arrogant excess' and 'heart-disease', stem from the sharpness of the Qur'an's encounter with hostility – to which we must come – in sequel to the militarism after the Hijrah. For more than the religious issue 'messengers' had in mind was at stake in armed confrontations which developed their own passion.

Some readers would want to account for their sharpness of accusation on that ground and discount this feature as sober verdict on human nature at large. The point will have place in Chapter 4. Yet even if such animus has that circumstantial origin, it does not gainsay the broad Quranic register of humankind in thrall to *zulm* and wrong, prone to idolatry and brutally capable of the treatment that 'sends messengers away empty'. Moreover, that same Hijrah, to whose sequel we may attribute that capacity as now reviewed, was itself instigated by the heedlessness of the *balagh* the messenger brought and by the deep crisis into which it brought Muhammad.[16]

If *khilafah/* 'dominion' is thus far precarious in such *zulm*-prone hands, the question seems to follow whether the entire mission of prophethood to creaturehood is not in grave crisis.

V

What, then, should the historian, not to say the theologian, conclude? It cannot be that creaturehood-in-trust is a failed experiment. To think that way lie chaos and the meaningless. The world and history are no work of a 'jesting Creator'. What, then, in view of its 'serious' reality, could this crisis around prophethoods mean? Is there something incompatible between human nature and the 'guidance' that addresses it, between our given autonomy and the divine purpose? Who could ever surmise that prophethood had finalised its task or that 'religion had been perfected' (Surah 5.3)? 'Religion' might be 'perfected' but what of the chronic 'imperfection' of its human incidence on every hand? Did the long series of messengers truly reach a climax at which it had attained its happy terminus?

The questions are more than rhetorical: they are the steady disquiet of a historical realism about ourselves, evident so legibly in the perspectives of time. As in the parable, there seems to be something evocative of refusal in the very advent of the messengers.

Perhaps it is the nature of law and claim that they are thwarted by that in human nature which greets them as dubious. A frequent 'evil' in the Qur'an is that of *zann*, false surmising, the harbouring of 'suspicion' which was often the precursor of *zulm*. The term, occurring as verb or noun or otherwise some seventy times, is reminiscent of that aspersion in the Biblical story of 'original' temptation: 'Has God said . . . ?' with its implication of some dubiety about divine intentions in the ordaining, and conditioning of human tenure in the world. It calls into question the very integrity of creation and of human liability under prophethood (Genesis 3:1).[17] *Zann* is in line with the insurrectionist umbrage of the husbandmen growing resentful of their constraints.

It is also squarely in line with Abraham's query (37:87): 'What are you supposing about the Lord of all being?' in challenge to the 'supposition' behind the idolatrous worship of his kinsmen. Elsewhere those who cavil about Muhammad's preaching and dismiss his themes of judgement and duty are told 'they do but conjecture' or indulge in vain guesswork

(6.148). They 'think evil thoughts of Allah' (48.6) but the 'conjecture' (10.36) they use deserves no trust, is no assurance of truth. Deluding 'suppositions' were a residue from the *Jahiliyyah* Islam was dispelling and these clinging habits of crude obfuscation should be recognised for the folly they are. The steady struggle of the *balagh* with self-deceptions of the Quraish measured how pervasive and insidious was their capacity to harbour 'wrong measures of God' as *ahl al-Zann*, 'the people of the surmised'.[18]

The upshot for both Biblical and Quranic Scriptures and for theologies there derived is that prophethood is in crisis in the very arena of crea-turehood, the realm of its relevance and its mission. Why it should be so is the central Scriptural question, after that of Allah over all, on which it bears so heavily. If 'You will be My people and I will be your God' that 'glory may dwell in the land' was the defining purpose of the Bible's 'first covenant', why should the story have so far miscarried in exile and disper-sion? If 'the aim of the Qur'an is man and his behaviour, not God', and 'God's existence, for the Qur'an, is strictly functional', has there been vindication in commensurate terms?[19]

The more seriously Scriptural faiths take the great positives of their vision for, and verdict on, the destiny of human entrustedness in and with the natural order of responsive sciences and sequential cultures and civil-isations and, by these, the vast dimensions of cumulative history, no less seriously must they take the dark discrepancies evident in the negations that vision/verdict have so long undergone.

That prophethood emerged into such crisis in its long encounters with human nature and that this nature should have proved so far dubious, obstructionist, devious and wayward – these are problems indeed, and not to be escaped except by forfeiture of faith's integrity and, with it, of hope and courage in theological belief. Is there something incorrigible in the human situation so that Scriptural 'education', 'reminder', 'admonition', and 'direction' are somehow a futile exercise? Must a sober realism conclude that the ends and means of Scriptured revelation are sadly at odds?

The trust we have in texts sacred to our faith communities has to under-take the issue in the dilemma into which they came in the very pursuance of their sacredness as both theme and story. It brings the 'sympathy' we have so far found towards 'a parting of the ways' where the dilemma becomes at once more obvious and more anxious.

Chapter 4

A Parting of the Ways – The Drama of History

I

THAT THERE ARE 'SYMPATHIES' IN CONTRASTS is obvious enough when the central issue causing them is the same but given divergent answer. The three previous chapters have traced the single Semitic, scriptural theme of a created order made susceptible of human management-in-trust and of that trust summoned by prophethoods into a directed, tutored fulfilment of autonomy thus pledged to the divine glory. Comparably, whether in Bible or Qur'an, that prophetic office found itself in prolonged experience of a humankind chronically resistant to the vocation and perverse with the trust. Prophethood became a cumulative register of travail and 'burden', undergoing the harsh consequences of an unwantedness that brought frustration to its message and dismay or despair to its bearers. The divine 'means' in words – to convince, persuade, recruit and achieve the human concurrence – seemed to fail of its divine 'ends' in ordaining the 'deputy-ship' on which all turned – and that by explicit divine intent.

In their perception of this situation the Qur'an and the New Testament take radically contrasted courses in response.[1] The Qur'an's was the Hijrah, the deliberate quest for the deployment of power, despite the earlier clear and exclusive mandate for *balagh* and despite its own question: 'Do you think that you can compel men to believe?' (Surah 10.99) addressed to Muhammad himself.[2] The New Testament's response lay in a studied renunciation of power and an impulse for the saving principle of redemptiveness, identified in the measure of 'Christ crucified'. Great controversy turns in both areas on the antecedents in either case and on the interpretations that told them in their respective communities, some of which we only come to it in the following Chapter 5. Here the task is the exposition of the answers in either, and how, in their utter disparity,

38

they were united as relating to a common divine/human ordering of a creation-in-trust.

The issue at stake might be had in the words of Paul to Romans: 'Be not overcome of evil, but overcome evil with good' (12:21). Each, Qur'an and Gospel alike, were set to ensure that (negative) 'not overcome'. They would differently conceive of the second, more exacting (positive) that might 'overcome the evil', whether by the force that fails in 'overcoming' or 'overcomes' with unsubdued remainder, or by a redemption that left nothing unmet. What, we have to ask, is the measure of 'the good' which effectively 'overcomes' the evil? The 'evil' thus far is a verbal thing. It is what the Letter to the Hebrews called 'the contradiction of sinners' (12:3) using a rare Greek word *analogizomai*, meaning, exactly, hostile 'language' rebutting the 'saying' of the word-bearer. The Qur'an in many places makes almost a refrain of that encounter – 'They are saying . . . say thou.' Whether there or in the Gospels that verbal confrontation steadily threatens, on the public side, to pass into more than verbal exchange. What then does the word-bearer do? Have the 'word' speak in other language, as Jesus had long been doing in ministries of healing? Or, realising that the issue of his words is steadily passing into a crisis around his person, take countering action? If so, what action, congenially with the words thus far and with the message they bring? It is useful to take the Quranic answer first, while holding in mind how the two situations agree as being 'the place for an answer'.

II

Its shape in the Qur'an would seem to have been forming by the logic of the years around 619 of Muhammad's *Sirah* or 'word-career'. There was something in his situation akin to that which kindled the prayer that ends the *Te Deum Laudamus* in other liturgy: 'Lord, in Thee have I trusted; let me never be confounded.' For – as Tradition narrates it – he was by then being very sharply 'confounded' in the seeming fruitlessness of his mission. The 'word' of the One, and omnipotent Allah was being refused in the name of non-entity deities whom the Meccans falsely invoked. Like the 'one who had learned' in Isaiah 50:4 and thereby given to carry a message 'ripe for hearing', he had incurred only calumny and reviling.[3] How was the contradiction, in such harsh terms, between his 'truth' and their 'falsehood' to be resolved?

That painful questioning was made the more urgent by his increasing loneliness following the deaths of Abu Talib, his uncle and stout protector and of Khadijah, his wife and mainstay in vocation. Perhaps Mecca as his first locale was not to prove the scene of verbal success. Prospecting outside it, at least in the ill-fated venture up to Al-Ta'if, proved painfully barren. The only promise, and that not yet a sure one, lay in the interest shown by men from Yathrib during a visit to Mecca, when they had requested a preacher to come their way. When, the next year, a deputation returned and entered into a compact with Muhammad to afford him sanctuary, we may conclude from the Tradition that it represented what his perplexity logically, if not deliberately, sought as an answer by which 'non-confounded' he might be.

It was a drastic 'migration' on four counts. It would involve a seeming abandonment of Mecca, the decisive locale of his mission with the Ka'bah of Abraham's rearing and the environs of his personal call. Secondly, it would entail for most of his disciples a rupture of their tribal bonds and a venture into the 'bond' of religion alone – major crisis for them all.[4] Thirdly, there was much potentially precarious in the prospect of the Yathrib reception, seeing that the offer of sanctuary had been made only in the name of some Yathribites with goodwill towards him. These *ansar* – as they would come to be named – or 'aiders' could not ensure the welcome of the whole population. Fourthly, if not immediately apparent, the new venue would come to mean the end of the long powerlessness of the preaching years in Mecca, the prime period of 'defenceless' religion, left behind in a radical shift of character and definition as the price of a perplexity resolved and a 'rescue' from impasse ensured.[5]

Given how crucial the Hijrah was both in the pondering and the effecting, it is surprising that it seems nowhere to have been explicitly commanded in Quranic words. By dint of the chroniclers of the *Sirah*, we can locate two proximate references to the event and the miraculous preservation of Muhammad and his father-in-law companion Abu Bakr in the famous cave incident, thanks to the diligent spider.[6] Those had to do with physical risks. The deeper essential risks around those four issues proved also well survived and vindicated. The new 'religious' bonds availed well to discriminate the tribal ones. A new minority element would prove more than viable in its new haven – so far so that Yathrib would be renamed 'Medinat al-Nabi', 'the city of the Prophet'. The defining decisiveness of Mecca could in the sequel be at least partially retrieved. Notice would in time be served that migration from it had been in no way abandonment of it, nor of its vital significance.

It was around the fourth factor that – depending on how the factors are assessed (which is our core concern) – questions painfully persisted. 'Powerlessness' would come to be a thing of the past but its being so would radically affect both the ethos of Islam, the themes of the Qur'an and, because of these, the historic perceptions of Muhammad.

At all events and on all counts, Hijrah was a pivotal event, apt to mark the outset of the Islamic calendar at 622 CE rather than a date of birth, or the occasion (unknown) of the Qur'an's first mediation. By long range and inter-faith assessments, the migration from Mecca to Medina has the significance that calendar tells. For becoming empowered in steadily more political terms, Islam was transformed into what, hitherto by criteria of its first Meccan *balagh*, it had never been. The transformation came to be definitive for all its centuries, only perpetuating the thirteen Meccan years in the Medinan form of contrasting 'empire'.

To be sure, the mediation of Qur'an to Muhammad continued but it had a new temper and a new content, becoming concerned with the physical campaign and a running commentary on its vicissitudes, the recruiting of its resources material and personal, and the ordering of its management in prisoners, ransoms, booty and martyrs.[7] A new will to enmity entered into Islam which had not been there before. Pre-Hijrah, there had indeed been round and urgent language against the sins and ills of idolatry and a moral passion against infanticide and other *zulm al-nafs* in the pagan order. That religious intolerance developed into the passions of battle. What had been at stake between Allah and Meccan society became also what was at issue between the armed camps of either.

Of course, the situation was mutual. The Quraish had every reason to be more concerned about Muhammad 'at large' than when he had been within their own urban scene and subject to their vigilance – a vigilance only still about the impact of his words. Muhammad established in another abode, pledged to his protection, was a more suspect entity, one now liable – as he had not hitherto been – to press his purpose in the armed terms that would range two bases against each other over the terrain between. Their hostility, already proved implacable in respect of the preacher, would inevitably become aggressive against a dangerous party that had eluded them. That party would counter them in a mutual joining of the quarrel between them. So much the logic of the Hijrah ensured, but the consequences for the future expression of that original 'Let God be God and He alone' would be profound.

The power-equation brought its own implicit demands of 'hardness of heart' when arts and feats of war became 'the argument'. Courage to fight became proxy for will to witness and, with it, the snare of thinking these were one and the same. Did not the word *shahid* suggest both one who 'witnesses' and one who dies – and the one who dies perhaps, as such, the one who kills? The Qur'an passed into a more strident tone. The resolve military engagement had to kindle had also to override misgivings drawn from human frailty, fear of death, apprehensions about widows and orphans 'rawly left'. The shift can be readily measured in the transitions of a single word, *fitnah*, meaning whatever tempts – and so tests – the human spirit. These, of course, were one thing in the Meccan scene, quite another in the Medinan. The earliest Muslims in the former had to contend with 'persecution', the customary lot of despised minorities exposed to adversarial power and enjoying none themselves. With the onset of hostilities, that kind of *fitnah* becomes instead 'timidity' in face of martial claims. Muslims are no longer 'persecuted' in the first all vulnerable time. Their adversities are now those of war and campaign, on 'the suffering end' of things in war's differing terms. Being, perhaps, made casualties 'tempts' them to resist their leader's claim to their allegiance but they will only not be renegades in being ready volunteers. Later as victory ensures, *fitnah* becomes the 'sedition' to which successful causes are subject by those who conspire to undermine them. There are examples of these 'trials by base traitors' in the *munafiqun* of the Qur'an – of whom there were none in the Meccan years.[8] Persecutions attend minorities, seditions beset what invites the enmity or the envy of those who still oppose it.

These features were the necessary price of the 'manifest and great victory' which Medinan Islam attained.[9] Mecca at length capitulated. By its own surrendering logic. Allah was vindicated as more powerful than its pagan deities who had conspicuously failed to better Him in battles. The keen failure of *balagh* – in the impasse which the Hijrah had addressed in its own different terms – had been totally reversed. Mecca had yielded.

But in what terms had Islam been received? The question belongs with Chapter 5. What matters here is that religious faith had been historically fused with power, its means and ways, and that, therefore, something had happened which – at least in respect of its inner assurance – was quite without precedent and would find perpetuation down the Islamic centuries as the telling model of a faith's legitimacy.

III

Precisely for that sequel and its long commendation to the counsels of religions, it is important to have the legitimation clear. The Hijrah, for all its 'Be hard with them where-ever you find them', was not sheer belligerence for its own sake. All that Yathrib becoming *Al-Madinah* symbolized was in the cause of the Meccan *balagh*. It was held to be the valid implementation of the divine quest of human means, via power, after word had failed. The lesson was that, if there is to be integrity, there must be this measure of intolerance. Incompatibles, when persistently proved such, must be subdued. There can be no honest exemption of the order of faith from the aegis of politics. Religion is right to equip itself with rulership. Prophethood was not called only to 'suffers fools (and pagans) gladly' but – at their charge and cost – to terminate their folly with the conclusive 'witness' of power and the necessary sanction of régime.

The validity of doing so derives squarely from the worth and meaning of the message. The more critical the word, the more warranted the régime it takes up in its name. In appreciating Islam this must always be kept in mind. Medina was/is on behalf of Mecca and in its name. Of Meccan priority in the scheme of things there can be no doubt, both historically and essentially. Mecca had been evacuated by the Hijrah, only to be promptly re-instated there by the change of the old *Qiblah* toward Jerusalem to convey all *Salat* toward that *Umm al-Qura*, 'mother-city' of the faith.

Hijrah, both by its personal challenge to the individual Muslim and in its definition of their Islam, gave proof that the thrust of the preaching about divine Oneness and human *khilafah* could brook no compromise. The Meccan faith must have its way and its sway. The 'reckoning', which was always proclaimed to be with Allah in line with the *balagh*, would come eschatologically 'in the end', but would come historically in Medina's 'manifest victory'.

It is possible – as some have done – to surmise that there may have been discernible 'trials' of compromise between the Quraish and Muhammad. Before all became so far embittered there was the puzzling matter of 'the Satanic verses' on which only obscure light is thrown by the Tradition. Does Surah 53.19–23 imply that a modus vivendi was available to Muhammad, perhaps concerted by his uncle stressed by the tensions among kin and clans – a compromise whereby he would concede to the Quraish their plural worships, if they acknowledged the supremacy over them of his Allah, making his Islam a sturdy monolatry not an exclusive monotheism?[10] If so, it did not succeed. 'They are but names', 53.23 insisted – human 'inventions', non-entities Islam could not, would not, abide. If there had been a parley, Muhammad emerged from it steadfast in his *la ilaha illa-Allah*.

The second occasion – it might be argued – was at Al-Hudaibiyyah when Muhammad came, by mutual agreement unarmed, on his second bid to do pilgrimage at the still, *de facto*, pagan Ka'bah he held to be *de jure* Abrahamic. Might this measure of negotiated 'tolerance' have been sustained, seeing that on his first bid for access he had been well armed and now had agreed to come, vulnerable and dependent on Quraishi good faith? Something similar had been implicit when he had agreed that 'Muslims' reneging back to Mecca from Medina would not be returned to him, while he would return new *muhajirin* acceding to him – a ruling which much dismayed his faithful ones, as did his acceptance to sign the treaty merely as 'Muhammad ibn 'Abdallah', without his *Al-Rasul* title.

That was an empty gesture by the Quraish. For the whole treaty-making at Al-Hudaibiyyah had been a tactic anticipating final victory. It had no elements of permanence and was so soon overtaken by the climax of their surrender.[11]

The two 'compromise' episodes, if we rightly think them such, only confirm what the two cities symbolised in those post Hijrah, pre-victory years, namely a faith requiring a necessary intolerance in its loyalty and a legitimate statehood in its cause. Both cities had their place in the affirming and confirming of Islam, and neither without the other. By their alliance, 'Lord, in Thee have I trusted' had its 'Let me never be confounded' for its satisfaction, and the genius of Islam would be known to the Hijri centuries.

IV

It may seem odd to write of 'a parting of the ways'. For there is no evidence that the New Testament scenario played any part either in the logic or the event of post-Hijrah Islam, nor that 'the suffering Jesus as the Christ' was in any way present as a precedent being consciously rejected or ever positively applicable. 'Isa had been raptured to heaven and so retrieved from the hostility his mission aroused. That divine intervention made clear that he had needed it, in that clearly he had not pre-empted it by evading, or defecting, action on his own part. His readiness to have been a victim was plain enough in the very necessity of his rescue. Jesus had never read himself in anything like Muhammad's situation so there was no actual 'parting of the ways'.

However, in the formation of the faiths of Scriptures there most emphatically was. For some twentieth-century faith-negotiator, 'Muhammad and Jesus on the road together' might be a slogan[12] but 'the road' was never historically trod as ever being the same road.

The crux lies in the theme of 'Messiah' so central to the New Testament's portrayal of Jesus' ministry and so far absent in the Qur'an's perspectives. Though regularly the Qur'an speaks of 'Isa (Jesus) as 'son of Mary, al-Masih' the 'anointing' is meant as referring to his status as 'messenger', not in any way incorporating the sense of the word that gives definition to Christianity itself, namely 'the Christ of God', 'Redeemer of the world'. Al-Masih, in that sense, is excluded from Islam's reckoning which is in line with the exclusively verbal, tutorial and legislatory form of Allah's relation with humankind in the given order of creation. Or, in the framework of any 'husbandmen parable' there are only 'messengers'.

The New Testament sees the Messianic vocation of Jesus as worked out in the day to day setting of his preaching and teaching ministry, his itineraries in Galilee and beyond, his comings to Jerusalem and the scenes of healing and compassion along his road. These all had to do with anticipations confusedly present in the popular mind – anticipations which stemmed from the long heritage of Jewish hope belonging to 'the land' and 'the kingdom' as these belonged in the mystery of 'covenant and people'. The contemporary context of Roman rule – and oppression – only made those hopes the more wistful and excited.

Jesus' ministry could only fulfill them by disabusing them of illusory political dimensions such as those most ardently held by the Zealots of the time. The teaching, caring ministry gave sign of a patient gentle Messianic quality – one which, for that very reason, could not fail to head into hostility and dispute because it so far disappointed. On other grounds, too, it incurred adversity for its characteristic by-passing of familiar 'establishment' notions of Scriptures and their 'official' inter-preters. There was a freshness and a spontaneity about Jesus' commendation of 'your heavenly Father's' immediacy of relevance to human need and hope, as 'One who knows' and 'numbers all your hairs'.

For all the differences of time, locale and temper, we should discern 'a certain sympathy' – though with contrasted issue – between Muhammad's experience in Mecca and that of Jesus in the Gospels. Resentments grew in either case against what was perceived as inimical to tradition, disrup-tive of complacent ease, and fit to be opposed as uncongenial or pretentious. There were deeply local and popular factors in either case tending almost inexorably to rejection and disesteem.

The contrast, if we read respective Scriptures rightly, lay in that the adversities of Muhammad were taken by him as inducing the Hijrah and the process towards 'the political kingdom' which would bring power-success' to his preached message.[13] Those of Jesus were taken by him into the very definition of Messiahship and thence into its realisation in the self-giving of suffering love. The very evident onus there is in this contrast we defer to Chapter 5. For the case either made – and makes – reaches far into the nature of God and perceptions of humankind.

Despite contrary reading, it seems evident that Jesus deliberately turned away from Messianic patterns, whether those of the Zealotry that would militarily unseat the Romans – as the Jewish Revolt decades later would attempt, or those of the ascetics who would withdraw into the desert in piety to await an eschatological hope. Jesus mingled readily with 'publi-cans and winebibbers', not disdaining neophytes of Rome nor forsaking human joys. Occasions 'by force to make him a king' he evaded (John 6:15) – something his popular following would joyfully have done.

Yet it is clear that Jesus had evoked high potential visions that could easily miscarry. Matthew 11:12 says:

> Until now the kingdom of heaven suffers violence and men of violence take it by force.

The 'violent' verb and noun are very harsh – 'plunder', 'seize', 'violate' almost, and denote an exercise of force born of excessive passion – some-thing 'the kingdom' undergoes, *not* what it itself is doing.[14] These were zealous activists bent on diverting Jesus into seizing on their own mood and totally to militarise his own mission. He did not do so, by deliberate repudiation of what he saw (in Quranic term) as *fitnah*, a trap and a snare denying the authentic Messianic call. 'Until now' must be read as serving notice on this clamant delusion that it had no place in the days ahead – as it never had in the authentic past. Hopes are often best fulfilled in being firmly denied.

The ultimate 'handing over' of Jesus in the garden of Gethsemane may well belong in this context of Messianic will in Jesus. Was Judas, by a sane conjecture on our part, seeking by his action to confront Jesus with an unavoidable decision by 'the kiss' that identified him in the darkness? Judas, who may well have been a zealot before, or still, may have reached a final despair about ever having been a disciple of Jesus by that effemi-nate business over the 'woman with the ointment'. What had such puerile futility to do with 'the Christ of God'? But if even he, this delaying, folly-indulging, Jesus were at length faced with a situation he could not baulk, namely deadly arrest, might he not at long last become a fighter, retaliate and usher in the longed-for riot that would initiate a saving rebellion? This seems a surer reading than the hint that Judas merely coveted 'thirty pieces of silver'. What were they to him?

It did not happen so and when Peter, with similar logic, drew out a sword, Jesus halted all belligerent ideas and accepted to be arrested – after which there would be no averting the climax.

Things enigmatic remain in the story but what emerges, both from the logic of the whole ministry and from the subsequent reading it had in the nascent Church, leaves no reasonable doubt about 'the way that Jesus chose and went'.

There is no need to trace again the pressure of events in ministry toward this climax. At every point, something like incipient 'crosses' develop between Jesus and the priests, Jesus and the leaders, over, for example, the Sabbath, divine forgiveness, the authority of texts, the status of publi-cans and 'Gentiles'. They were 'crosses' in that there was a will to silence him, murmurs of ill-will towards him, urging counter-action going far beyond mere tacit disapproval.

If, inside the consciousness of Jesus, all this adversity was being pondered in the setting of Messianic vocation, how close at hand to his mind was the precedent of suffering prophets from whose loyalties with truth that dream of 'Messiah' had come? The route seems clear from the contours of 'the suffering servant' in Isaiah to the garden of Gethsemane. 'The cup my Father gives' was how Jesus read vocation, as the very circumstances of its pursuit in place and time presented it to him, against the familiar backdrop of the travail of the prophets, the prophets from whose hope and story the Messianic theme itself had come to birth.

Throughout it has been right and honest to study the 'sympathy' between Muhammad's encounter with adversity and that of Jesus heading into his Gethsemane in the single element of an antipathy sustained. It has, however, at this point, to be qualified by the crucial contrast in the two sequels. Muhammad's Meccan trauma argued Hijrah and Medina and all ensuing from these. Jesus' travail moved on to the Cross. There had been – in both cases – a 'not being overcome of evil' by dint of insistent fidelity. Whether there would be any 'overcoming of evil with good' would be what either, in their total contrast, would have to show.

To underline that open question and to esteem the contrast truly, it is useful to note how the great Muslim sociologist Ibn Khaldun (1332–1406) argues in his Prolegomena (*Al-Muqaddimah*) that prophets must certainly organise and inspire *asabiyyah*, or 'collective spirit', or 'group ardour'. On this ground Jesus ought to have let those 'men of violence', those 'enthusiasts', have their way and give them rein. A prophet needs 'prestige' among his people 'until he achieves the religious organisation God intended for him!' Otherwise there is no achieving due superiority.[15] For the New Testament community gathered to Jesus' 'prestige' it was a different order conceived in the sorrows through which it had passed in following him.

V

How community was inseparable from faith had been assumed from the very nature of the 'witness'. Muhammad had striven to recruit disciples in Allah's Name so that *Shahadah* ensued in *Ummah* and the *Kitab* found its *Ahl*, the very 'people' of its bonding. Likewise for the Gospels it was axiomatic that the 'Messiah' would find, or found, Messianic community. So it certainly proved in the New Testament story. What is noteworthy is how closely the pattern of defining origins was reproduced in the ensuing society.[16] The nascent Christian community proved as suffering-identified as its Lord.

Indeed there was in the initial persecution of the newly minted Church a clear continuity with the animus against Jesus which had culminated in the crucifixion. Saul's hostility to Stephen and those pioneers in Damascus only maintained the verdict Caiaphas had pressed against Jesus. So much was evident in the meaning of his experience on the Damascus road, as presented in his friend Luke's narrative in Acts. 'Why are you persecuting me?' was the pointed question, so apposite if the hearer's very venom concealed a struggling mind already half convinced against its own logic by dint of Stephen's dying and other factors. Much mystery clings to the drama but that surmise has strong psychic warrant. 'I am Jesus whom you persecute', when the whole antipathy had been against the new community.[17]

That solidarity between Lord and people – if we rightly read it – was surely perpetuated in the sequel of three centuries of the suffering Church, victimised by Roman oppression, living under the likes of Caligula and Nero and unready to challenge their *imperium*, as well as totally unable.

That founding condition of the Church has endured as its most fitting *métier*. When the 'Christian' word was first invented by jokers in Antioch it was linked with deliberate irony as denoting something despicable (Acts 11:26). The only two other uses carry a similar ignominy (Acts 26:28 and 1 Peter 4:16). Paul, in Philippians 3:15, read this situation as 'fellowship with the suffering of Christ', as also did 1 Peter 4:13. It was out of a sense of 'Messianic inclusion' that they explained this solidarity. The suffering Christ was not merely the Master they preached but the one they emulated in reading their own condition in the world and the vocation it told. It translated into their own social relationships the perception of God that had told itself in Jesus' words: 'One there is who forgives . . .' They would do likewise, by something of the same self-expenditure, in their dealings inter-human in the world. For those who believe themselves 'redeemed' are thereby called to live as 'redeemers', and only they who accept not to retaliate effectively 'redeem' thereby and draw the sting of enmity.

This inter-play between the saving story of Jesus and their conforming esteem of it is impressively evident in the way in which the New Testament literature is itself the creation of the New Testament Church. In this quality, there is no 'sympathy' at all with the Qur'an – a Scripture which its *Ummah* possesses but which it did not itself compose.[18] One can only account for the New Testament as document by dint of 'New Testament' as life. Those Gospels come about as texts because a community had memories. They are memories it had vital need to enscripture because it was widely spreading in geographical expansion and coping with the lapse of years. There would have been no ground for Gospel writing without communities concerned to know, because they were so distant from Galilee in Corinth and so far from Gethsemane in measure of time. Only a missionary Church could have necessitated – and produced – its own text.

The same factors obviously account for Letters educating this dispersed society in its own ethical life and the social expression of its faith-heritage. Dispersed it may be but it is not 'un-Messianic' and its essential character means its nurture by a monitoring apostolic authority, set as it is in a bewildering Roman and pagan world.[19] A centrifugal web of discipline belongs with a centripetal community in which the many are one by the necessity that they are many.

This self-expressing quality of the Church across human frontiers, thus mirrored in its founding documents, stemmed only from its being a preached thing. Its reach outside its Judaic birth into its 'Gentile' embrace was the direct sequel to its own content as 'historic redemption'. The hurdle it took in surmounting that long and stubborn Biblical divide was possible and achievable only by virtue of the inclusion it was able to read, of all and sundry, in the scope of 'Messiah crucified'. All other versions of the Messianic meaning had confined themselves to 'Israel', whether as political zealotry, or Essene-style asceticism, or apocalyptic waiting. The embrace of the Cross was represented in its very shape as the gesture of divine inclusion and the unclinched hands, thrusting no fist into the air.

Ibn Khaldun, at one point, opined that Christianity was 'not a missionary religion', because it pursued no *Jihad*, though later he agreed that it preached its *balagh*.[20] His instinct was that faiths were not inwardly fulfilled in the absence of a power dimension in their name. Words, with no will to bring 'régime', were hardly self-consistent. Only an activism on their behalf could satisfy and vindicate their content as idea and truth. The spiritual telling was bound up with the political taking.

By contrast, nascent Christianity, for three centuries, was innocent of power. Jewish Christians of that generation withheld themselves from all participation in the tragic Jewish Revolt of 66–70, despite great pressures on them to share the Jewish reading of the 'sacred' obligation and perhaps offset the seeming 'treachery' of their participation 'in Christ' with 'Gentiles'. In that respect, they were clearly exercising a deliberate choice, though – that context apart – one may argue that the Christian 'peace-mind' was simply their option-less situation, Rome being so overwhelmingly entrenched. They were powerless anyway, so that there was no virtue in their acquiescence.

That case has often been made by Muslim commentary. Then the quite contrasted Arabian situation fronting Muhammad is evidence of the more ultimate vocation he was given – that of effectively subduing a feud-prone pagan society to single political control. That Jesus never enjoyed such a scenario becomes an aspect of his being 'pen-ultimate' to the Apostle for whom it was politically possible to attain and realise the ultimate reach of prophetic destiny and, once and for all, demonstrate its final, definitive shape.

The Qur'an, in its Meccan/Medinan sequence, would certainly be witness to that conclusion. For its whole ethos stands with it. In that different sense, it might resemble the New Testament, in being not the product but the register of its own mission. It effectively documents its own genius but does so in quite explicit terms of its own. Its human instrument was that of one recipient. It may be fair to say that the collective genesis of the New Testament as literature is, indirectly, the surest witness to 'the Messianic secret' according to Jesus which its community worked out in the world. For, without that origination in life and death in Galilee/Jerusalem, it would never had been.

The 'power-innocence' of the pre-Constantinian Church as more than mere *de facto* 'powerlessness' seems clear on further grounds. There, as one scholar writes:

Nowhere do we hear anything of the voices of oppressed peoples who gave vent to their wrath against Rome's rapacity and destructive fury, in the manner of the King of Britain in Tacitus (Agricola 30) . . . nowhere the voice of painful boredom with which Rome's own writers and poets . . . recommended to the prudent the surrender of the capital city and flight to the country.[21]

Rather, there belongs with the Letters of Apostles a quiet presence in a harsh world, with inner resources of patience and long hope. The heat, for example, in Galatians is reserved for matters of faith and moral loyalties. Where Paul is passionate it is because he is vigilant, and vigilant because he is anxious. Even in private with Philemon he handles slavery itself in the context of a *de jure* equality persisting 'in Christ'. If there is a 'tolerance' of what cannot be changed, there is tenacity in the light of it and sincerity enduring it. It was not an enmity-making faith, except in respect of those who disputed its Christ, for whom and with whom came the language of 'We beseech you . . .' or 'Ourselves your servants for Jesus' sake.' Otherwise, for their inward mood, their social order, they had 'let this mind be in you which was also in Christ' and 'Let the peace of God rule in your hearts,' where the allusion was not to an ever fleeting thing they had to guard, but a strong 'garrison' in charge of them.

To know it so is not to romanticise. There were blemishes aplenty in its story and dark shadows in its society. Yet it survived and grew in spite of Rome's rigours, for three arduous and turbulent centuries and weathered the strains its embrace of 'Gentiles' entailed especially after the devastating Fall of Jerusalem and the desperate demands of drastic self-preservation it induced in the Judaic community negotiating a parallel dispersion. Its defining formula 'in Christ' was its security until, for all its controversies of faith-definition and its human frailty, it looked attractive enough to a pagan emperor to suggest its enlistment into his imperial ambitions. That fateful turn of its privations early in its fourth century faced it with burdens and temptations that would quite transform its self-perceptions. Their entail takes its altering destiny into the chapter following, where 'sympathy' with Islam in point of political status and the power dimension would also be dramatically changed.

Chapter 5

Sympathy Engaging with Antipathy – Power and Faith

I

THERE ARE RELIGIONS AND PHILOSOPHIES which deny that our existence is truly historical existence. Events do not significantly happen nor do persons signify. All resolves into the vacuity of something all inclusive out of which we and time are only illusorilly caused to seem and mean. Semitic faiths, by contrast, are committed to the seriousness of history, of personhood and of ethics in the social order. So far is this so that the world is read as a venturesome entrustment in our human hands, there vested by a divine intent that was no empty 'frolic' of some 'jesting Creator', but a calculated risk, an enterprise keeping faith with itself via the amenable, humanly manageable patterns of this 'good earth', on all these counts a mindful habitat.

This we have traced in the two Scriptures where all Semites learned it so. Their sense of divine ends invested in human means, and their perception that human means prove sadly awry in that quest with divine ends, we followed in chapters 1 to 3. The perceived agency of prophethoods set to monitor this ever-liable creaturehood, through obvious diversities, is their common tribute to the dignity of our *khilafah*, the shared proof of the Creator's mindfulness. Both Bible and Qur'an are alert to what the latter calls 'the whisperings in the bosom of humankind' (Surah 114) by which that dignity is subverted into self-betrayal in the pursuit of *zulm* and wrong. These are the 'sympathy' mutual to both Scriptures and their peoples.

However, Chapter 4 studied how sharply they parted over how this subverting might be ended, be brought instead into a due *islam*, understood as positive retrieval into divine purpose and fulfilled creaturehood. The Qur'an sees the remedy in given revelation, enshrined in a structure of law, ritual and régime by which a genuine *taqwa* or God-fearing-ness, is realized. In its interior progression into the New Testament,[1] the Bible – while sharing the role of law and discipline – finds the crux of vital human transformation of 'thoughts and intents of the heart' only in what it calls 'redemption' at the price of the vicarious love that enables forgiveness at its own cost and with it an 'undoing' of wrong and a 'righting of the self'.

This meant 'a parting of the ways' in quite radical terms (if we ignore chronology and focus on how either faith began) but it has not cancelled the sympathy which alone is the ground of the contrast. It is only because they have thought alike that they reached occasion to differ. Faiths that disavow 'historical existence' disown all that gives the issue meaning. That there is a mutual onus either carries concerning the other's version of the 'remedy' remains the clear responsibility of their co-existence.

Tragically, however, the history of their co-existence has darkly impeded and intimidated that responsibility.[2] Either has come to seem – or to be – a breeder of enmity towards the other. New Testament faith has felt an Islam that rode roughshod over all it most dearly cherished concerning whom it endearingly called 'Our Lord Jesus Christ'.[3] It reciprocated with scant recognition of the kindred territory we have traced and with obtusely ignorant skirmishes around the central figure of Islam.

Much that is at stake here turns on the vexed issues of Scripture readership to which we have to come, on 'the writ of readers' to discriminate to reach 'right measures' of what they read.[4]

But looming through all these tasks is the matter so evident from the previous chapter, namely the role of power in the things of religion, the puzzling nexus between politics and belief, or *Dawlah* and *Din*. For it was here that the origins of Quranic and Christian faiths were so dramatically contrasted in the power-equation of the one and the powerless genius of the other.

II

Realists are bound to ask: How can religious faith ever think to absolve itself from the power dimension, inseparable as rule, sovereignty and governance are from the human scene? It might endure powerlessness if insuperable factors condemned faith to it, but would duty not lie in reversing such vulnerable condition by timely seizure of power? Could it be less than treachery not to equip itself with the sinews necessary to have its truths prevail beyond all neutrality? One need not be cynical to ask, as many have done, What is the use of Gethsemane? – 'Put up your sword: suffer it to be so' – and have the sole ikon of discipleship arrested and led away to die? Was not the robust belligerence of Medinan Islam exactly the right polity – to prevail and be magnanimous only thereafter, fortified in an unconditonal surrender of the other? If faiths are about what demands all and takes all it demands, is not such attaining militancy no more than their self-consistency?

> You who reject faith! I do not worship what you worship, nor do you worship what I worship. Never will I be a worshipper of what you worship, nor will you be worshippers of what I worship. To you your religion and to me mine.[5]

The logic of the Hijrah is already latent in this early Meccan Surah. Muhammad was not minded to leave the things he so insistently rejected in control of his society. A counter-militancy against what was effectively entrenched would be the proof of such conviction. Such militancy must obviously sustain its success, once achieved, by keeping firm hold on the exercise of power in an abiding hegemony it would never forego.

Thirteen centuries after Muhammad's decisive establishment of Islam in a recovered Mecca and a victorious Medina, the first Prime Minister of the newly created Pakistan made the point in moving 'The Objective Resolution of the Constituent Assembly'. The year was 1949.

> The State is not to play the part of a neutral observer, wherein Muslims may be merely free to profess and practice their religion, because such an attitude on the part of the State would be the very negation of the ideals which prompted the demand for Pakistan.[6]

No! The State exists to ensure more than the 'practice of religion'. 'Neutrality' is no part of its *raison d'être*, which was – and is – to embody and fulfil Islam in and by the entire panoply of government, law, jurisprudence and political authority. The notion of 'neutrality' around any diversity of religious faith, ritual or practice, reduces religion itself to purely 'private' criteria of its range and claim and precludes what only its identification with the state and its political order can safely and duly afford. Centuries of 'Christendom' since Constantine's adoption of the Church into his imperial scheme have proceeded until modern times on a thoroughly Islamic legitimation of the political order, in many different forms through the Holy Roman Empire and the nation state, Catholic or Orthodox or Protestant. The great Augustine somehow divined that the old Roman formula of *arma et pietas*, by which Roman Emperors 'divinized' themselves as embodying the sanctity of Rome in that of their own person, could give way to a 'Christian' Emperor's enshrining of a Christian baptism alike of *arma* and *pietas* – a formula which would warrant the later concept of 'the divine right of kings'.[7] There could be no 'neutrality' about faith in the age-long assumption, alike of Islam and Christendom, that it should embrace and pursue political hegemony both as its preserve and its sound preservation.

Do we conclude that – by these lights – the 'sympathies' earlier examined have no antipathy to overcome, seeing they have both, and for so long, been thoroughly politicised systems?

It must, therefore, now seem naïve to argue, as is here proposed, that Muhammad's thirteen years power-free in Mecca and the Church's three centuries in catacombs *do*, in their essential priority in both cases, make the present case for the 'neutrality' Liaquat Ali Khan excluded from the Pakistani mind.

Surely a quite extravagant logic, realists will say. There was no 'neutrality' in either case. The Meccan Qur'an is thoroughly combative in word and passion, the Medinan Qur'an in action and conflict.

> Woe to those whose hearts are hardened against the remembrance of God – they are in open error. (39.22)

> He it is who has sent His messenger with guidance and the religion of truth . . . Those who are with him are sternly against deniers of the faith and compassionate among themselves. (48.29)

> Their deeds are like the darkness in the deep of the ocean, under cavernous waves, billow upon billow, and dark serried clouds rearing above – a darkness so intense that a man could scarcely see his own hand in front of him. (24.40)[8]

'Be hard with them where-ever you find them.' The Qur'an is ready to be implacable against unbelievers, both in this world and the next. No 'neutrality' here. Nor is any to be argued from Meccan 'powerlessness' – the very factor which demanded power-possession.

How then can it be argued that Islam's first Meccan experience has any relevance to its present self-analysis? The contemporary case required in this twenty-first century must await Chapter 7. Meanwhile what of Meccan situation there and then? Was it not utterly ripe, in its obduracy and its wrongs, for the treatment it received?

The question turns – as then so now – on the meaning of 'neutrality'. For clearly it conceals two quite disparate meanings that urgently need discrimination if Islam as *balagh* is to be true to itself as essentially unco-ercive. The sort of neutrality Pakistan's Constituent Assembly was exhorted to repudiate was not an 'indifference' to truth *per se*. It was, rather, a concern to be in the open forum of personal conscience where it might honestly co-exist with other faiths. Therefore it must ensure and enjoy political rights in non-exclusive terms.

Islam in defining origin had no such protection. Pagan Mecca not only denied it but marshalled the very opposite in venomous persecution only the Hijrah and sequel would reverse. Precisely by that circumstance Islam had found itself with an authenticity Medina would change for ever.[9] It had been conviction in heart and will alone – a total 'non-neutrality' set against an adverse hostile non-neutrality radically threatening it – but quite unable to subdue it. Need Islam fear its fate in a like exposure to vulnerability – not now through rampant hatred but of amicable diversity?

That question bears strongly on the constant Quranic emphasis on human *khilafah*. Must not this entrustment mean that all decisions, including the central religious ones, are freely given into human hands? The possibility of its being employed 'doing corruption in the earth' was present when it was promulgated, as God's intended gift to us. Given – to be sure – to be devoted to divine ends, but only voluntarily so. Otherwise, how would its prophetic education be so urgent? We have to concede, within its revealed terms, that the possibility of 'the secular' exists, the option of *khilafah* distorted to our own unworthy ends. Otherwise, how should 'idolatry' happen and be so reprehensible?

In Surah 7.172 our *khilafah* was interrogated and Allah's question was: 'Am I not your Lord?' The passage envisaged all the generations of human history somehow assembled in a single, simultaneous audience. They all prospectively replied: 'YES, indeed, we witness that it is so.'[10] Thus, the passage, as we saw, rules out any excuse of ours blaming 'our forebears as leading us astray'. If we perverted our *khilafah* we did so ourselves.

This fact, central to Quranic humanism, of the trust of personal liability for the self, with that self meant for divine employ, must surely include our personal liability to fulfill it by responsible discernment of the religious structure of faith and action that properly equips us to that end. No faith allegiance then can be authentic outside such exercise of *khilafah* in surrender to it. Many might argue that, for long centuries, religious identity was axiomatic, a thing of birth and heritage where no conscious will had part or place. Yet Islam, on two counts, sought to end that tradition. Its pre-Hijrah *balagh* was a summons to personal decision and its Hijrah, as we have seen, was a testing ground of such individual initiative. Further, the Qur'an, as it were, took up the case for *khilafah* as having religious decision inside its purview, by pleading that Islam itself was *din al-fitrah*, 'the religion proper to human nature'.[11] That doctrine, namely that our *khilafah* was only properly exercised by submission as Muslim, must also mean that *khilafah* did and should adjudge between religions, even if, outside Islam, it was judging unwisely. The claim that its mandate went soundly in only one direction meant that its mandate might be subject to the criteria – doctrinal and moral – addressing human nature. The appeal to human nature, itself so far at stake in *khilafah* in ways we have seen concerning divine risk, might then come into legitimate debate where, in effect, Surah 30.30 placed it. Perhaps we then have to conclude that crucial to all religious allegiance is an honest assessment of ourselves. Only so are we truly *khulafa*' (pl.) as human trustees in Allah's world.[12]

III

The theme of the true religion coinciding with human nature rightly judged gives a gentle irony to the large theme of *dhimmi* status which Islam accorded to 'peoples of the Book' and faiths it could allow to persist. The system arose directly from the integration in classic Islam of faith with power and belief with sovereignty. The irony lay in that it allowed other faiths to subsist precisely in forfeiture of the political dimension which Islam alleged to be crucial to being a 'religion' at all. It 'covenanted' with the tolerated to enjoy protection and the security of their 'religious' rights (worship, ritual, child nurture, family law etc.) only on the basis of a renunciation of such notions as equal citizenship and a role in the state.

It meant their deliberate inferiorisation, as faiths it was oddly stubborn of their adherents to cling to, once the final religion had been disclosed and was so freely accessible to them. If the contract by which in this way they subsisted was broken their security was forfeit. The precariousness varied from place to place and century to century according to the moods and attitudes of its supervisors.

This *dhimmi* system was a freedom to 'survive' and, as such, a gentler alternative to outright persecution. It might even be argued that it threw minority faiths back on their own spiritual resources. But these it also atrophied in serious ways, not only by the humiliation of the *jizyah*, or tax, but by the denial of all reasonable occasion for faith's self-expression outside its own families. It confined the churches to being inarticulate entities whose core beliefs could have no express relevance to the world at large. They had occasion neither to recruit nor to grow but were resolved into static communities, disallowed new church-building and forbidden the public possession of their most cherished symbols. If it could relate at all to the world of Islam – as some élitist figures contrived to do – it was from a social inferiorization, while the pressures to Islamise were all the time heavy on both economic and psychic grounds. All in all the *dhimmi* order of things was, for those enduring it, no more than a palliative of Islam's rubric of perennial political authority uniquely in its hands, and supposedly necessary to being a right 'religion'.

It might be urged that such critique of the lot of *Ahl al-Dhimmah* assumes concepts of religious tolerance which could never have been viable in those early and late medieval centuries, neither in *Dar al-Islam* nor in Christendom. In either realm the faith-power equation was complete and went unchallenged. Power had an indispensable role and religion must control it. The point is fairly made, but what the *dhimmi* structure meant for those under it was only the measure – in their experience – of a situation hazardous for Islam itself. To have minorities

56

languish was in no way to serve Islam in its own integrity. It was sadly the measure of a larger – and inward – compromise of religion.

This brings us to the heart of the matter – the dilemma of any religion in purporting to be what that word essentially denotes, namely a commit-ment to an ultimate integrity in the love of truth and the care of justice and compassion. Only such integrity is the full measure of that *khilafah* the theisms affirm whereby we humans, by our own active recognition, are 'under God'. For, whether a faith is 'theological' or not, this inclusive liability as all-embracing, is what 'religion' means. The old Latin wisdom, of which Islam would certainly approve – *Non Deus nisi Deus Solus* – (or 'Not God at all unless God alone') as the meaning of *la ilaha illa Allah*, captures precisely the nature of religion, whether 'theological' or not. It means the loyalty that neither deviates nor defers outside its inclusive focus of obligation, whose right to its submission is inalienable.[13]

At first sight it might seem that an exclusive access to and exercise of power on the part of 'religion' so defined would be mandatory. For how else, if not in control of the political order, could it ensure the ultimate loyalty? *Non Deus nisi Deus solus* would need to be enforceable.

The assumption is wrong. For there is that in the exercise of power which requires it to seek, not only its own perpetuation, but its own ulti-macy. It chafes at being merely the instrument of something more ultimate than itself ostensibly employing it. Its ends must be its own. Its own inner dynamic conspires against its due subordination. This, as history evidences, is only the more likely when its 'employer' is religion. For then it has the supreme warrant to usurp what it serves. 'In this sign conquer' Constantine understood to be his destiny at Milvian Bridge when he adapted the Church to his banner. But whose 'conquering' would it be? 'The more we serve the greater cause,' the more we have 'the cause serve us.'[14] To cry *Allahu akbar* is the more passionately to think *Islamu akbar* or to merge either cry with the other, if militancy is meant. The power-dimension then offends against our human *khilafah* as that which must, indeed, be summoned, but may not be over-ridden or coerced. Is it not from that quality of human *khilafah*, the crucial organ of 'religion', that Surah 2.255 rubric must derive? 'That there may not be compulsion (*ikraha*) in religion', seeing that 'religion' is, by definition, the most inher-ently volitional thing?

Given, however, how indispensable governance is to the well-being and due order of society, not to say the business and traffic of the nations, it is clear that religion – in its very capacity beyond the reach and province of power – must have due relation with it, but by a nexus that has reli-gion without compromise and power without its besetting lusts. Political theory readily recalls Thomas Hobbes' argument in *Leviathan* urging that power must be 'absolute', for only so would it suffice to save a world of incorrigibly competitive humans from reducing society to a chaos, its 'life nasty, brutish and short'. His view may have had a realism about the reach of envy, greed and sin within what the Qur'an knew as 'the bosoms of men'. It was, in fact, a realism not discerning enough in its assumption that these, the ills that such absolutism might serve to rein in, were far from being the only threats to common good, or that absolutist political power would not itself succumb to them.

Moreover, would such dire restraining of them in thus 'not being over-come of their evil', ever remotely begin to 'overcome evil with good'? Power might serve to keep that option open. It could never achieve or fulfill it. Redemptive business lies elsewhere. Addressing moral issues in society, and in private persons, by the artifices of power can at best attain only partial remedies. This is because there are reaches of *zulm* and wrong and guilt in them that admit, externally, of only a modicum of correction, justice, righting, deterrence or whatever it be that law adjudges or contrives. The inward issues of guilt, grief, suffering are where 'damages' are far other than any legal calculus can assess or satisfy. This truth of evil is not merely what we have *done* deed-wise, but who we *are* to such deeds-prone. There is not only what law can indict in the state's name but what self-awareness must accuse within. Such is the very nature of *khilafah*. It is implicit in all we have studied. It belongs with the Qur'an's own verdict: 'It was their own selves they wronged,' and with the psalmist's cry: 'Thou requirest truth in the inward parts' (51.6). That is a realm which must address politics but yet transcend it as something its means cannot reach.

IV

If 'religion' – as the term itself indicates – is the mentor of our being human in these ultimate terms, deep lessons seem to follow. The first must be that its place in politics and power, alert to how these will maximize its own temptations, has to be that of a critical conscience – a role which will be impossible if there is total inter-alliance and near identity of *Din* and *Dawlah*. For then its capacity to advise, address and accuse the State will be lost in the vested interests of its own monopoly of the power structure. The most impressive feature of the classic Hebrew prophets is that while they cogently confronted and challenged the seats of power, they never occupied them. We find Isaiah, Amos, Hosea and – most heroically of all – Jeremiah present with faithful conscience in the courts of kings but ever only in their prophetic role. So far was this so that in some cases they incurred the charge of being 'traitors' to the State by the very vehemence of their care for its righteousness.

The distinction they categorically made, and symbolized, between 'the things of God' and 'the things of Caesar', did not in any way mean that these were two separate realms where 'God's' had no business with

'Caesar's' and 'Caesar's' no reckonings from 'God's'.[15] The distinction stands only in what is inherent in the nature of either and belongs with the very meaning of human *khilafah*, namely that God's realm, being uncoercive, is not power-ensured and that the realm of politics, being power-based, needs a constraining conscience whose criteria it cannot impair or deny – criteria safe and immune from those which power itself wills to exert.

'Not power-ensured' about God's realm may seem a strange assertion to the traditional Muslim mind. For the transition from Mecca to Medina seemed to demonstrate precisely the contrary as the unambiguous validation of religion as power and of power as religion. How else could the pagan order of the Quraish have been brought to a decisive end, seeing how perversely it has been power-sanctioned? The logic seems irresistible but only if we exclude that Quraishi perversity from any human *khilafah*. For it had happened as a phenomenon in that very context. Was not 'Am I not your Lord?' (7.172) a genuine and far from rhetorical question, a question that might have the wilful answer No! – the answer the Quraish had made. The whole thrust of Muhammad's mission turned on a real, and in no way ignorable, human *zulm*. They could not be exonerated by 'their forefathers'. For these also according to the passage had pledged' to Allah the 'submission' they had also disowned. That 'only God was God' could be a summons because it was at stake in the human scene and in no way axiomatic. Only by its being at genuine risk could Muhammad have a mission. For the *khilafah* on which it turned had been given to 'all the progeny of the seed of Adam'. Its once-for-all acceptance in the womb of time conceded how right it was: it did not make its honouring assured.

Do we not have to agree that what is loosely called 'the secular' – not anything outside God's order but only inside it via our will to set it there – has to be acknowledged as entailed in our *khilafah*? Or, in Christian vocabulary: 'Hallowed by Thy Name' is no plea, no aspiration, no intention unless 'unhallowed be' is not the contrary these must override. Then an interesting realisation follows, namely the 'secular' widely obtains, by its own right, however wilfully we have handled it in bland or brutal vulgarity. We do not have to make 'the sign of the cross' on entering a laboratory, or think it a mosque before an experiment will work. Many areas, especially in the sciences, are of this almost necessarily 'secular' character by virtue of their nature, but only, therefore, the more deliberately to be hallowed by the intentions, distinguished from the procedures, we bring to them.[16] Viable 'procedures' are what make for our *khilafah*. Our 'intentions' are what take it – and them – in hand. This necessary 'secular' character of things material, however, is no license to be irreverent, wonderless, ungrateful or exploitative.

The attitudes which belong with 'hallowing' are thus – by right religion – extensified through all 'secular' workings that do not, operatively, require them but are only duly sane or safe with them. Such 'extensifying' can only happen if, somewhere, what it cares about and brings is somewhere 'intensified' in 'the sacred' known and loved as such for its own sake. These – mosques, churches, times, places, active symbols – may *seem* to be separate from markets, banks, factories, oil-wells, aircraft and computers, but only so for their sake. Contrariwise, pieties, devotions, holy times and places *may* become mere superstition if they do not translate their meaning down into the working world. For 'humankind is in a middle state', called to consecrate earth in Allah's Name, called to celebrate Allah's Name in earth's plentitude.[17] Such is the true meaning 'secular' and 'sacred' have as the full range of our 'dominion', where *laborare est orare* and 'to reign is to serve.'

V

The tragedy with religious faith, however, has almost always been that, instead of 'intensifying' the factors set to make the operationally 'secular' the steady realm of such Godward celebration/consecration, it has accentuated factors that connive with human supremacism – the endemic evil of all human identities, the will to rejection of 'the other'. For human diversity is beset with much potential ill-will, deriving from territory, ancestry, race, nation, security, suspicion, strange cultures, history and memory. With these and their tragic trend into malignity, religious faith all too readily conspires – if it does not expressly kindle them into action. For faiths belong inextricably with all of these in the long centuries of their moulding of culture, conceptualising of land, shaping of language and readings of history. All have been liable to veto their own best insights concerning 'one mankind' in the pursuit of their own political interest or their collective supremacy.[18]

This propensity to yield themselves to enmity or darkly accentuate, aid and abet forces demonic in society is the more likely the more closely religious faiths are identified with state power or demand exclusive control of it.[19] For then they surrender their duty to be its radical conscience, its urgent judge. The Hebrew prophets – as we noted – who knew that situation well, could never have been the honest prosecutors, the cleansing ministrants they were, had they been wielding the power they indicted.

Sadly, thus state-wedded or empire sanctioning, it is not only that faiths forfeit their right, and their ability, to be power's accusors. It is further that they become themselves embroiled in the passions and interests, the temptations, of the power equation. Something injurious happens to their own integrity. Every attentive reader of the Qur'an is aware that change has happened to the very fibre of being Muslim in the years after the Hijrah. It is then, almost exclusively, that we find some thirty of so allusions to the *munafiqun,* and their *nifaq,* the 'dissemblers' and their 'hypocrisy'. Under adversity in Mecca there was no occasion to pretend allegiance. For only sincerity (*ikhlas*) sustained it. When, however, Islam became 'a strong factor' in the scene, it might become prudent, cautious, even urgent, to adhere to it. For conflict involved even would-be neutrals in suspect terms. Why had they not 'come on board'? Wars have a way of cancelling the very notion of 'neutrality', – religious conflicts most of all. Making the stakes martial meant that believing might well become more a calculus of discretion than a conviction of heart.

The Medinan scene was heavily cast in those terms. Hence came the need to distinguish between *muslimun* and *mu'minun,* the former adherent 'muslims', the latter believing ones. In later external campaigns, 'Umar was styled *Amir al-Mu'minin.* To have been 'Commander of the Muslims' might have been a less assured role.

This fragility of allegiance minus conviction, as the liability war-sanctioned faiths run, was evident in Surah 49.14–17.

> Desert Arabs say: 'We have believed'. Say: 'You have not believed. You should rather say 'We have become *muslims*', i.e., 'We have surrendered.' Faith has not entered your hearts . . . Believers are those who, having believed in God and His messenger, do not doubt further but strive in the way of God with their possessions and their persons. Such are the ones who are truly sincere.

Then it emerges that these recruits had imagined they were doing a 'favour' to Muhammad himself.

> Tell them: Do not consider your *islam* a favour done to me. It is God who does good to you in guiding you to faith, that is, if what you say is sincere. God holds the secret of the heavens and the earth, and everything you do is open to His sight.

It was doubtless part of that Medinan, and subsequent, situation that readiness to be martially involved was the acid test of believing conviction. But ought a *religious* faith to incorporate this non-religious element of battle into its spiritual claim on the disciple?[20] There was no element of it in the *Shahadah* which was about God and His word-bearer, himself summoned by no more than *Iqra'.* In effect, sincerity shifted its essential ground from 'the intent of the heart', and so doing caught up the 'intent of the heart' in the possibility of criteria quite extraneous to faith in God, such as self-glory, valorous reputation, and 'the spoils of war'. These could only darkly poison the very well-springs of sincerity.

Moreover – as is evident in late Medinan Surahs – the vigilance that set due watch on *nifaq* could make its practitioners the more alert to deter suspicion. It was not a situation conducive to open integrity, given and recognised. And if due attainment of power be the necessary hallmark of faith – and activism in the campaign to such power the test of discipleship – will not the subsequent faith/power equation become victim to the same logic when dispute arises over faith-content? Such a structure will be the prey of its own formula. So it sadly proved in the long history of Islam, and comparably in that of Christendom.

The *Khawarij*, disowning the faith-expression of early Caliphs, did so in the form of political challenge. When the Shi'ah segment in Islam diverged sharply from the evolving Sunni expression, it perforce did so in the power realm.[21] Hence the disappointment and then the unquiet years of Caliph 'Ali. Hence also the Umayyad trickery against Hasan and more foully still the Massacre of Karbala'. Islam would seem to have condemned itself to the bitter politicisation of all its religious truth issues. And so it remained until Sufism by its third century taught Muslims an activism that was peaceably religious and religious only, Muslim as Muslims had initially been in Mecca.

The Christian Church had that 'activism of word and spirit only' for three defining centuries. Lives had to be risked for faith's meanings, not because these were minded for empire, but because empire was ill-minded against them. When Constantine after 313 aligned empire with them, faith's sense of an unfamiliar power-wield slowly took possession of 'the intent of the heart' and many features, later instinctive to the Islamic system, supervened in mixed fortunes with the Roman Empire, the Carolingian 'holy' version, the medieval Papacy, Byzantium, the Hapsburgs and the modern nation state, all applying in their sundry forms the *cujus religio/ejus regio* principle. For all the centuries of adversarial relation after the rise of Islam, it was a curiously Islamic principle. Indeed, one might say that the inter-enmity stemmed precisely from the fact that both *Dar al-Islam* and 'Christendom' were religio-political expressions, so that strictly doctrinal and intellectual themes between them were never free of power-interests to find congenial encounter in their own right.

'The divine right of kings' has a strangely Islamic ring in that it was two-wayed – the power claimed *over* 'subjects' was the obligation due *under* God, whose alone sovereignty was. The king, like any human 'caliph' was 'in a middle state'. This was no defence against absolutism if the 'upward calling' was ignored. The order of power, in its own realm, was bound to the same principle of *khilafah* in the order of common existence. Power, however, with its impulse to self-preservation, has always been more self-pretentious than ordinary folk. In any event, the fusion, in 'Christendom' and post-Hijrah Islam, of power and belief, of politics and faith, meant that heart-conviction became rule-allegiance and thus liable to the forfeiture of its soul-integrity.

It was naïve, in the Anglican tradition, for theorists like Richard Hooker of *Ecclesiastical Polity* and the early Gladstone – naïve about human nature – to think of a steady, serene identity between subject and believer, between citizen and communicant.[22] It could never tally with the tensions inside faith itself, nor with the emotions latent in exploring them. Quietists like John Bunyan could only then participate by years in prison in the patience of their sufferings – a circumstance grimly to indict the 'polity' that had it so.

Slowly and painfully faith, deploying power in polity, had to concede the genuine role of the 'secular', and forego exclusive control of the State and its writ of law, not renouncing the obligation it must still carry. Rather that obligation would need, on faith's own sanest ground of liberty with truth, to search co-operation with agnostic or even hostile minds. The nineteenth and twentieth-century curbings of 'ecclesiastical polity' were well served, if not prompted, by the sure warrant of its New Testament shape. That there has been a genuine ministry of 'secular' insight to the religious mind is evident enough. Honesty compels its recognition as a proper discipline for faith-people to undergo. For its quest after intellectual integrity, its care for human liberty, for conscience and realism about religion's corruptibility' – all these are within the private *khilafah* of every human soul, whose prime bestowal, according to the Bible and the Qurʾan, was antecedent to the coming of any revelatory law or historical theology.[23]

This readiness on the part of religious faith for a ministry to it of 'secular' philosophies means no abnegation of its witness to, or vocation within, society at large. Moreover, large cultural factors – language, history, architecture, tradition and art – blessedly persist to invite retrieval from neglect and mediate their faith-origins the more religiously, thanks to the tonic of such 'secular' co-existence, the openness of which may be salutary for other faiths' traditions in diaspora presence. Indeed, some continuity of the symbols of the faith/power nexus may be a useful reminder of what it once, however ambiguously, denoted, namely that political power, whether of empire or kingship, was no 'law unto itself' but properly subject to spiritual accountability.

Power-girt faith in 'Christendom' terms, post-Constantine, long exhibited the evils *Dar al-Islam* had known, namely the tyranny of power over moral discernment, the near atrophy of critical judgement, the compromises of conscience in approving what deserved to be indicted. Most deadly of the compromises of faith in the pursuits of power were those of the Spanish conquerors and settlers in their brutalities against Amerindians. These were too seldom confronted by a moral indignation like that of Bartolome de Las Casas, a Dominican Father and later a Bishop in Mexico, who startled the whites with: 'Are you not obliged to love them (the 'natives') as yourselves and to be trusted as true subjects of the Castilian Crown?' His *Short Account of the Destruction of the Indians* became a beacon for the likes of Simon Bolivar more than three centuries later.[24] Laws might be enacted against the worst crimes of the settlers but they availed little against the licence of the powerful.

In their different idiom the chaplains of the East India Co. in British India struggled under the constraints of the 'official' Church Order embarrassed by the heavy compromise their power sanction set upon their spiritual integrity.[25] When nationalism moves into imperialism it is idle for romantics like Disraeli to cry: 'We wish to conquer the world with angels at our head.'[26] That sense of destiny is far from angelic. There has been no religious faith that could stay 'pure and undefiled' in exclusive partnership with the organs of political power. Yet good governance is a priceless boon to human society and a vital dimension of the common welfare, a sphere of liability from which no religious faith can be exempt. Where do we find the clue to this riddle?

Does it not lie in our human-wide *khilafah* – a common endowment knowledge of which we owe to religious texts, but never confined to their human communities, never discriminating in its creaturely incidence but commissioning all alike? Unilateral monopoly of it in the realm of politics and power is only to generate contention as to 'the pure version' of the faith that does so.[27] We then have 'demons at our heels' and such faith becomes an enmity-generating identity, only rescued from the menace to itself and all by ceasing to monopolise.

But, so doing, it will not abdicate. Its moral writ will run more duly by partnering in this 'caliphate' with other faiths and none whom, thus, it has not ousted from Allah's 'caliphal' gift in them. In those terms even a so-called 'secular state' may be read as a theological reality.

Chapter 6

Holy Writ and the
Writ of Readers

I

KEEPERS OF ORIENTAL MANUSCRIPTS IN ancient universities might seem oddly so named, their charges being neither mobile nor dangerous. 'Minders of Oriental Manuscripts' would be a more fitting title, covering both the ministries old texts require of the caring attention that preserves and the studious attention that consults. Librarians as such are not theologians, nor is exegesis in the business of 'keeping'.[1] The 'keeping' function with its fine techniques anticipates the reading concern and serves the scholar's task.

The gentle irony in this situation belongs most squarely of all when the 'kept' are sacred Scriptures. By virtue of their status they have received meticulous care as due for inviolate preservation, so far so that sanctity did duty for intelligent possession. 'The Holy Bible' was revered for its own sake as 'the Word of God' due for reverential handling quite unlike all printed things elsewhere. *Al-Qur'an al-majid, Al-Mashaf al-sharif*, were titles of honour which set apart the Islamic Scripture as the utterly sacrosanct document of Allah's revelation. Its Surahs and verses were the supreme referent for its people. 'People of the Book,' we might say, became apt description in both cases.[2]

Such was the standing of 'Holy Writ'. 'Writ', however, is also an ironic word. For while, on the one hand, it means this 'sacred written-ness' from God, it comes also to mean a form of words by which the recipient has an authority all his own, a power to act, maybe to make an arrest, discharge an office, or attain a purpose. How could 'Holy Writ', we might ask, ever resolve into a formula which gave itself away in such terms? Familiar concepts of its own documentary mandate would seem to preclude it from passing thus into some 'writ of readers'.

Yet, with all due deference, this is precisely the case as what must happen by the very nature of 'written-ness' and by the status of 'reader-ship' this intrinsically bestows. The moment we have 'wordedness' in legible – as distinct from oral – form, mental cognisance of its textual character becomes the first and last condition of its relevance, the corollary of its existence. The 'holiness' of 'Holy Writ' in no way escapes this situation: it is only the more sacredly involved in it.

When, at the outset of *wahy* as usually identified in Surah 96, Muhammad had the inaugurating command: *Iqra'*, as is well known, it meant 'Recite . . .' as vouchsafed words inscribed in heaven, a text in no way his own. All was vocal. He was not invited to 'peruse'. The same verb, however, also means 'peruse' even in such usages as 'he read the palm of his hand'. Giving voice to the Qur'an remains the prime duty the Muslim has with the Qur'an, in the *tajwid* by which the 'chant' savours and celebrates its Arabic diction, its rhymes and assonance. Yet that liturgical duty cannot displace the steady task of 'reading' as the student must, paying initial tribute to grammar by parsing but aiming to satisfy the Book's own urgent plea: 'Will they not *reflect* on the Qur'an . . . ?'[3]

Thus the whole Qur'an exists by the necessity of the vocal becoming the textual and that textual requiring not only the 'reciter' but each 'reciter' in turn becoming the reader in the inclusive sense of the word. This situation, with appropriate differences, is discernible in the Hebrew Bible, where the clarion cry of the prophets is: 'Hear the word of the Lord . . .' Moses, the lawgiver, comes down from his Sinai with 'the tables of the Law', written on stone. The reader's sense of thus being 'under divine authority', which is itself couched in words imperative, only makes the heeding role the more urgent – and there is no heeding that can dispense with due reading. Even when Hebrew Scriptures become more involved in narrative the history these contain – since story has the same revelatory status as coded law – makes a discerning readership still more crucial.

When, in Christian Scriptures too, we find that the Gospels only eventuated as documents out of an insistent human demand for the words of Jesus as, hitherto, only verbal memory contained them, the liability of readership had the double duty of heeding them as thus registered *and* of taking into careful stock the process by which they became so. Still further away are we from mere verbalism in the case of the New Testament Letters. For here a pastoral and apostolic education of newly recruited believers is proceeding as the very matrix of the literary transaction. There could be no clearer index to the necessity of readers placing themselves imaginatively inside the human circumstances of that education. The ever present question 'How readest thou?' attaches critically to every kind and type of sacred writ, even where the 'Thou shalts . . .' 'Thou shalt nots . . .' of the most abrupt laws seem most categorical.

Whether we are dealing with 'the glorious Qur'an' or with 'the Holy

Bible' the text is addressing our common 'caliphate', not superseding it. We cannot well harbour a sense of Scriptures as if outside our sense of creaturehood within divine creation. Any theology of attention to either has to be an attention to both. For only within our liability thus to 'move and have our being' can we be intelligently summoned by directives or alerted to deviance as prescriptive in so doing. The entire Semitic mystery of 'revelation as Scripture' and of 'Scripture as revelation' means that readership and creaturehood are terms that pre-suppose each other.

Nowhere is this reality more evident than when, in the Bible, the personal pieties of the psalms and the intuitive lore of the 'Wisdom' writings with their 'proverbs' and epigrams come, seemingly uneasily, into the same volume as 'the law of Sinai'. For what thunders is also now what whispers: the stentorian has become the intimate. The private emotions of 'O God You are my God' are the more given to 'the keeping of Your precepts' in the social realm. Nowhere, perhaps, is the experience of being 'Scriptured' taken more into ardent selfhood than in the stanzas of Psalm 119. 'My soul is continually in my hand. Yet do I not forget Thy law' (109). The awful liability of the law ensures the heedfulness in the soul. He senses the urgency of the text in the very frailty of the self. 'I am a stranger in the earth. Hide not Thy commandments from me' (19).[4] Only so can he say: 'Thy statutes have been my songs in the house of my pilgrimage' (54). The Qur'an may not admit such private yearnings into the fabric of the text but something of what the psalmist meant by them finds expression in the love of calligraphy and the art of recitation.

II

Those skills, however, and the tribute they pay to the sanctity of the text are, in themselves, no substitute for the task of commentary, of *tafsir* and *ta'wil* that draw out or elucidate the meaning, so that we 'detect, develop or disclose' what is there which, otherwise, might remain obscure or be misconstrued. Since this task in respect of Scriptures is implicit in their very textuality, reticence about it or neglect of its necessity are no part of its true esteem. There has, therefore, to be 'a certain sympathy' in this territory between esteeming the Bible and esteeming the Qur'an. The calligrapher in either case surely serves and commends the task but, *qua* penman, does not discharge it. Likewise, the reciter or the citer unready for the more subtle caring about it on which every verbal medium depends. Revering the text means undertaking the perplexities and hazards that accompany all language usage, the issues that turn on words.

For 'sacred language', as Biblical Hebrew and the Qur'an's Arabic are held to be, allows no scholarly exemption from the onus of their textual employment as vocabulary, idiom, image, irony and diction. The integral role of Arabic, already noted, in the very standing and evidences of the Book as Allah's word, means that its matchless eloquence, as its supreme 'sign', can only be mediated in being redacted, either by the inferior Arabic of commentary or the non-Arabic of translation. These, even if successful, will be isolating meaning from its indispensable form, but only for that very meaning's sake.

That sort of issue attaches less rigorously to the Bible's Hebrew, while the Greek of the New Testament – for all the Pauline and Johannine tension with words – is known to be *koine*, or simple usage. New Testament Scriptures are happy in claiming no 'sacred language' status for their contents as eminently fit to be 'vernacular' anywhere. In any event, that Arabic of the Qur'an was always meant for being intelligible in the Arab scene and, therefore, was a credential which would be less relevant elsewhere, as evidencing 'a mercy to the worlds'. It is better for Scriptures to have their language 'sacred' most of all in the cherishing their contents enjoy when, as the Hebrew psalmist held: 'All the kings of the earth shall praise Thee, O Lord, when they hear the words of Thy mouth' (138:4).

Whether for translation outside its given stature, or for due discernment by its habitual users, kindred to its original quality when scriptured, such hallowed text will always be in the mental and spiritual trust of the community. All Scriptures are thus, we might say, domestically possessed. They belong uniquely where uniquely they belong, in a way different from mere national literatures. They have, by their very nature, generated insiders whose instinct for them they have themselves shaped. It is one such custodians fear is unlikely to be had when it is drawn into foreign relations. There is thus a problem for the psyche, as well as for the intelligence, in the whole business of translation and of alien study. Nowhere has this dilemma been more acute than for the Islamic community in the care of the Qur'an. It can only be overcome by being accepted as the necessity in being universal.

In this way the familiar phrase 'the people of the Book' is more loaded than is usually thought as 'two mutually identified' facts in religion. To whomever applied, it establishes a nexus between possessors and possessed that is formative either way, rather than merely descriptive. It underlines, alike for Bible and Qur'an, the significance of Scriptures as a 'canon'. This means how, in either case, the community undertook – and discharged – the responsibility for the texts as we have received them. That this must have implications,some of them perplexing for the writ of readers now, cannot be denied.

In respect of the Qur'an, it might be said that no 'canon' exists – certainly not in the sense of the Hebrew Canon devised by the Fathers at Yavneh after the Fall of Jerusalem and the loss of the Temple and its liturgy, nor of the Christian New Testament Canon taking some three centuries to decide its final mind. The classic view of the Qurʾan holds that its shape, its contents with neither lack nor excess, were final when the Prophet died – and could even have had the sanction of his actual approval. Nevertheless, there was a process of 'rescension' during the Caliphates of ʿUmar and ʿUthman which was finalised during the latter's reign, whose reported destruction of alternative versions took care that none survived to challenge what he finalised.

Much mystery surrounds that process and indeed the steady assembly within its community of the items of 'periodic' revelation.[5] It seems clear that Muhammad's death was, if not sudden, alarming enough to have taken the community by stunned surprise. Had there been occasion – in a continuous, ongoing enterprise of action and crises – for a studied attention to a compilation of texts, garnered from two cities over more than two decades? While it is clear that what was 'Qurʾan' was distinguishable from what was not in Muhammad's words – thanks to the recognition of *wahy* in its incidence, and assuming that such criteria of *wahy* were well sifted and attested in every instance – large questions remain for any absolute confidence in how rescensions moved to their final presentation of Surahs, *ayat* and contents in the sequences of the received text.[6]

The crucial point is that it could only have been a privilege and a task of loyal community, of community even vying to assert its local loyalties as textual formations came to cluster around particular locales in the rapid expansion of Muslim rule, whether Mecca, Medina, Damascus, Hiraʾ, or Aleppo. From their 'consolidation' by ʿUthman, the actuality of varied collections is not in doubt. Whence the chapter namings, the mysterious Arabic letters at the head of several,[7] the allocation to pre- and post-Hijrah as Meccan and Medinan – and all in a script not then bearing vowel signs or crucial diacritical points for consonants? Clearly, for that vital quarter century, the Qurʾan as long generations came to know it, was crucially at stake in the shaping of the first community. The indices – in quality of Arabic and 'signs' of recipience and genuine incidence of *wahy* – were all in the cognisance of that community of faith. If, as some western scholars have ventured to conjecture, the period of formation stretched even longer, that role was only the more invested.

Those qualities were certainly believed to be inherent, yet being sought and gaining communal recognition, only so they became the received Qurʾan. There was no 'Canonisation' in the Biblical sense: only this certifying process, this collecting and ordering, without which the historic Book, as such, would not exist. The communal hallmark of the process after Muhammad's death betokening its closure, can be seen as – in a different way – continuous with the text's own steady appeal for reception at its hearer's hands during its *tanzil*, with a challenge to outdo its Arabic or answer the steady appeal of its invocations, the very witness of wind and star, of night and day, of the embryo and the womb.

69

In this strange way, the Qur'an and Islam inter-depend. The faith has warrant in that its Scripture is 'the Book of Allah'. But 'the Book of Allah' is known so in the warrant of its people's faith. God's action is primary and absolute but the faith-awareness is its reciprocal evidence. God's primary action was of a sort (by its very policy for a 'scripture') to turn upon such awareness both ensuring and heeding the authority it must deploy. The sceptic may say that all is resolved into 'a faith in faith' – an empty gibe which, however, sets sharp question for religious integrity and, thus, for 'the writ of readers'. Before coming to it, however, it is sympathetic to realise how a very comparable situation obtains for lovers of the Bible.

III

Here, of course, the landscape is much contrasted and we are dealing with two Testaments in not always obvious unison. For purposes of their 'Canons' the 'candidates' were from a vast stretch of patriarchal and prophetic time, so deeply contrasting with the bare decades of the Qur'an. The Torah and the Writings, in any event, were likely to become wedded with the Oral Torah to yield the Talmud via midrash. Did the first century Jewish Fathers sanctify their Hebrew (and slightly Aramaic) Canon and the Alexandrian Canon in the Greek translation for their re-assuring solace in a dark hour?

As for the New Testament Canon, there was, indeed, a protracted process but only because certain 'marginal' texts, like 2 Peter and Jude, were for long in question. The will for a 'canon' stemmed from the desire to conserve a doctrinal quality free of divisive 'doubtfulness' yet hospitable enough to bring the Pauline and the Johannine alike into one purview.

The process was certainly the community agreeing a verdict on itself, on its scriptural identity, approving 'inspired' status but not, thereby, bestowing it. Far more significant, however, than this act of devising its own referent was the fact, already explored, that the community had been 'the womb of authorship' from the outset, in a way very different from the 'eventing' of the Qur'an.[8] The spreading Church, surviving beyond the first generation that alone had eye-witness memory, felt urgent need for scripted documentation. Hence the impulse to the Gospels giving written permanence to what, in oral terms, might become ever more fluid and precarious.

As for the Letters comprised in the Canon they, too, could not exist without a dispersion needing them from a recognized inner authority impelled to send them. Thus the double ethos of 'community dispersed and gathered' is self-evident from the Epistles no less than from the

70

Gospels. The Church gave being to its own document because it was its genius to do so. Yet, for its scriptural purposes, it decided, by canonization, that these – and not other – texts would be its definitive referent. It would have its designated identity inside these parameters.[9] Only in being thus 'Scriptured' would it know itself officially.

There is a comparable paradox then between the New Testament and the Qur'an, in that – in either case – the community validated its own validating document. The time cycles differ drastically but, in each case, a community accumulates its given texts, believes in their divine origin, sets them into a confirmed form and takes them for the ultimate datum of their faith. Tradition (*Hadith*) in Islam will develop extensively to throw vital light on the Qur'an's incidence but it will not come inside it.[10] The closure that excludes it – of the Qur'an – believed to have been first applied *ipso facto* by the death of the one recipient to whom all is owed, is also made by communal decision, so dramatically as to destroy all surviving elements that might, or might not, have diverged from its contents thus finally fixed. That 'eliminating' aspect of the Qur'an's rescension was more intensely exclusifying than the Church's making of 'rejects' in the shaping of its Canon.

There are, of course, deep disparities in the 'coming about' of those contents, whether by community genius or by single personal *wahy*, but the role of Christians and Muslims of the relevant years, in the delineation of what, in scriptured terms, delineates them is manifestly similar. They have not given birth to themselves but the birth they were given is certified by them – as was implicit in being a scriptured event inside the womb of words. *Iqra'* was thus itself a *Kunu*. 'Read' was realised as: 'Be . . .' and so continues in 'peoplehood with Book'.

Several germane matters also are present. Biblically are all Books of equal value, Esther as worthy as Isaiah, or Leviticus as Hosea? Ought Surah 97 to have some kind of priority over Surah 111, its holy summons over the other's grim malediction? Or Surah 100 with its passionate denunciation of violence and Surah 9's urging to it? Just as Christian exegetes have debated the claims of the Canon as esteeming the wholeness of the Bible for literary 'appreciation', or possessing individual books in their own right,[11] so do Muslims plead differently about understanding the Qur'an by the Qur'an. Heirs to what has been done once and for all by rescension and a Canon have the more liability, because of these, with what they are bequeathed.

Clearly, 'the writ of readers' is an exacting one, even deferring here to the next chapter the onus of new time and altered place. How is it well exercised, given how crucial readership is to the well-using of texts and ever the more so when those texts are 'holy Writ'? They have this 'privileged' status conceded, though not conferred, by their faithful to which these, just by being the faithful, have made themselves liable. How free may they become under their own constraints and, if not free, how honest? How do they at once sustain the privilege and yet read as if it were not there?

IV

There are immediately evident two areas of responsibility in this 'writ of readers' – the one internal, the other external. There are all the duties of scholarship between a reading historian and a reading theologian. For neither can be exegetes of that scriptured 'privilege' without the other. There is the external relating of 'the Book' to the fact that there are so many other 'privileged' Scriptures across the world. It is idle to disavow them on the ground of the prior warrant of our own. For they have commanded the heart emotions of multitudes and, for good or ill, have dominated the destiny of their societies for generations. Moreover, they do not concede themselves in any way disqualified to encounter rivals, seeing that, in every case, their criteria of authority are in their own keeping. The self-regard they receive from their 'people' turns on very discrepant accounts of what guarantees their status as 'inspired', but these accept no common assessment that would resolve the issues between them.

It is well known that this situation is acute between the Bible and the Qur'an, in part because of their 'sympathies' of theme concerning human creaturehood in earthly 'caliphate' and prophethood from heaven sent to guide it. That, however, has long been overborne by the heavy veto one has over the central theme of the other as to 'God in Christ' and the crucial dismay of that other in the later emergence of what purports to make it, at best, pen-ultimate and, at worst, superseded in the stakes of revelatory finality. There are, of course, numerous lesser 'bones of contention', around divergent narratives of patriarchs and only vexed compatibilities elsewhere, notably concerning the New Testament.[12] These exacting arenas of relationship are only the more problematic if we allow them also to be answerable to the 'secular' mind, as it would impinge on us both from the likes of Abu-l- ʿAla al-Maʿarri or Thomas Hobbes, for all their outward prudence in their own day.

The stresses of 'rivalry', at least for some minds, compel the question whether it is possible and loyal, to come – still with the contents of our Scriptures – out of the bastion of our dogma *about* them, in order to bring those contents from the sanction of their setting and assess them for their own sake? They could then be free for reckoning outside their 'charmed' character, no longer had in awe for that reason but hand in hand for what they told to minds un-awed. Scriptures would not then be read by us as if they were no longer such, but by us and other faithful (and any not so) in the neutral light of rational day or – maybe – in the dim shadow of human despair. Does meaning finally hinge on its auspices or on its credentials, on where it is found or on what it told?

If it be argued that for 'divine revelation' there can be no distinction between auspices and credentials, since 'inspiration' has made them one, we are back with the business of 'rivals' and doomed, in the end, to the incommunicable.

The import of Scriptures, evident in the 'word-policy' they employ and the whole reliance their faithful place in them, surely lies less in pleas for their status and more in transactions of comprehension. It is these that are impeded when prejudices, either has long had against the other, promptly intervene to cut off genuine connection with the themes or divert attention from them to minutiae liable to be productive only of persistent controversy.

Further, there has to be a mind for those around who respect no scriptural 'privilege' or are even appalled by the obscurantism to which its custodians will resort. Ways have to be found to set readership where its discernments need to be and away from disabling suspicion or no less disabling pride, whichever it may be.

Yet it is true that Bible and Qur'an have always been concerned about the standing which internally they possessed. It was vital for Muhammad to be able to insist: 'This is none other than a revelation imparted . . . ' (53.4): '. . . His servant lied not in what he saw . . .' (53.11). So there could be 'no taking issue over what his vision is'. Or for the Hebrew prophet to affirm: 'The Lord called me . . .' or 'this is the very word of the Lord'. Or for apostolic name and fame to underwrite New Testament language. There were always exigencies *in situ* when the Scripture was in the making, often in the Biblical world by men who had no dream that they were participating in what would become a 'Canon'. Muhammad's use of 'scribes' and the 'at intervals' character of his deliverances (17.106) indicate that he felt himself party to the accumulation of a text. In a hostile world, he needed all the under-girding such attestation could afford.

Yet, in every case, all that could serve to verify was on behalf of what was meant to educate. The 'how' of commission mattered only for the sake of the 'this' of mission. Muhammad was the means to the Qur'an just as the Qur'an was the means to the word-and-world purpose of Allah. Likewise with the Bible. Given that both Scriptures are now so thoroughly 'actual' in history, and given that this very rank-through-time carries the hazards of mere veneration or of impatient prejudice, must not priority for them lie in rescuing the end in them from the means?

That case is all the stronger in that, even while immersed in the struggle to be heeded, the hopes behind the text were ready to appeal to credence outside their own standing. The strenuous invocation, alike in Bible and Qur'an, of the sacred 'legibility' (might we call it?) of the natural order grounds corroboration of their words. These were especially prominent in the Meccan Surahs as a summons to truth. Or the Isaian contrast between the amenability of 'ass and ox' in their natural order to the will of mastery and the obduracy of the human species. The word is still that of a voice, a spokesman, but goes outside that category for its verity. It is a 'Listen to me' only in order to be 'think on this'. Even 'Holy Scripture' may go outside itself to find the case for itself. It suggests that its trustees might do the same the more to bring it home, appealing for itself by a logic outside itself.

So far does this happen Biblically that the private ruminations of a psalmist can come to constitute divine words. God finds him in searching why the world bewilders and oppresses him. The *tadabbur*, the 'pondering' to which the Qur'an also appeals, seems to require us to argue that themes which Scriptured 'revelation' claims to present – and present with all the warrant that status assumes and its custodians deploy – are alive outside it in the anxious pre-occupations of day-to-day living. 'Holy Writ' belongs with such curiosity, rather it invites it by a true persuasion towards ripe conviction.[13]

The singular virtue Scriptured faith-communities ascribe to their holy document does not exempt those communities from the mental liabilities or the spiritual burden of the one human scene. Even if their faith retreats, as it were, into a private precinct of security it will still be liable to co-existence with a world that queries why it did so and thus explicitly interrogates it. At some point the need to be more self-responsible will confront it in the traffic of issues not to be ignored. For what it thinks to isolate in a would-be fortress – if faith at all – has still to educate an open world, which means conversing with doubt on doubt's own terms. Is it not in the very nature of language that it engages with all its users? 'Holy Writ', in opting for words, has less escape than any from this predicament.

When, for example, the Qur'an observes about the Meccan pagans that 'they did not esteem Allah as He should be esteemed' it is a dictum that could well have come from a Plato, or a Spinoza, or a Feuerbach opining that 'deity' is no more than a projection of human aspiration. 'Right ideas' about God – being, ruling, causing, exclusive, inclusive, abiding, obsolete, ineffable – are the stock in trade of philosophy. The Qur'an uses here a very telling word for any philosopher – the verb and kindred noun *qadaru* and *qadr*, 'to measure, quantify, weigh, assess', so that 'proportion, sum, content, size' are known and proven.[14]

Here, then, in a single root word, theologians find their whole task comprised. It is a task which Christians among them would know must incorporate Christology, despite the Qur'an's own inclusion of that theme among the pagan ill-measures of God. This central emphasis on right 'measures' in theology, as the very crux of worthy worship and of compre-hension of the world, suggests that our Christian/Muslim task belongs squarely with them. Hence the concern of five foregoing chapters with where a right theology has to take us, namely our common faith about, and action in, the world of creaturehood at divine behest. That means, in turn, a close attention to the dark evidences of wrong and tragedy in that custody and what answer these might have from the divine sovereignty in whose realm of law and liberty they had transpired. 'Right esteem' of Allah must incorporate right measures of the human scene and story. The Biblical/Quranic theme of creation for the sake of creaturehood, and of creaturehood schooled by Scriptures, makes humankind the conclusive sphere where 'God in true esteem' can be known and told. *Haqqa qadrihi* has to be paramount over all else and to be the ultimate discipline of all scriptural duties.

Thanks to the classic understanding of its mode of verbal 'inspiration', Muslims have always found their deference to the Qur'an of a more literal and rigorous character than that brought by Christians to the Biblical text (though there has been a Biblical readership liable almost to Quranize the Bible). Muslims have often registered a perplexity that many Christians lack the textual mind proper to Islam.[15] These issues arise from disparity between us about how 'Scripture' came to pass in either case. An over-riding concern for *Haqqa qadrihi* can surely transcend these differences and the mistrusts they create, once we have realised that 'the truth of His measure' is why – and in our hands – those texts exist at all and that 'God in His right worship' is the sum and goal of all exegesis.

Acceding, then, to a tenable 'sympathy' between our Scriptures, despite misgivings over contrasted perception of their credentials, and setting 'God over all' as where we have to come, we realize how the 'privileged' status those Scriptures enjoy makes a 'privileged' role for their 'people' as their 'scripturists'.[16] It is a privilege, not for aggressive pride or dogmatic shelter or thoughtless citation, but only as an onus that engages us vitally in the traffic of cultures and the anxieties of the world. For only a divine Lordship that had incurred the risk of creation, a creation set under a commissioned creaturehood in its care, would have taken up also the risk of language. That readiness for words, with all their flux and fragility, their use or abuse, did not exempt itself from these by virtue of being 'Holy Writ'. Rather it left itself self-commended to the discerning patience of its 'people' whether in the margins where they set their readership or in the 'offices of prayer and praise' where all revelatory vocabularies belong. This had led us from 'externals' of right perception to the 'interior' possession of sacred language.

V

At once we have to reckon with that often elusive 'sense of the word', where dictionaries may only partly help and usage is always a shifting thing, or – if not shifting – exhibiting a strange facility to be ambiguous. The immediately preceding paragraphs might suggest at once the *akbar* in the familiar cry of the *Adhan: Allahu akbar.* It occurs in Surah 29.45 in the words: 'Remembrance of God is *akbar*' in a context about 'establishing worship' wherein is that which is 'better'. It is used elsewhere in making simple comparisons – a 'greater wage', a 'heavier requital', or, in 2.217 affirming that *fitnah* ('insurrection') is a greater crime/sin (?) than *qatl* ('killing'). No such *min* ('than') can follow *Allahu akbar*, since God never enters into feasible comparison, being 'exalted above all we can associate'. Yet *Akbar* without *min* became the personal name, descriptive of the greatest of the Mughal Emperors. As a comparative, grammatically, for ever without a superlative, what can it denote, unless a perpetual 'God is greater', disavowing all pseudo claimants to sovereignty, all idols and idol-makings in any and every culture, religion or political order? It is a magnificent principle, the very heart-thrust of Islamic genius: 'Let God alone be God!'

Yet what quality do we mean in this exclusive 'Great'? It cannot denote mere 'bulk' or 'mass' (as the *kabura* root might). Maybe only 'magnanimity' is right but that word may only repeat the elusive index we need. Can it include an authority that somehow awaits what it would deserve, that would be no longer great were it only tyrannical? Can it be a 'greatness' capable of the kind of paradox that would be unusual in the human realm where 'power' prevails and 'forebears' not? The necessity of paradox in a 'greatness' that is divine has always been axiomatic for the Christian tradition of theology. Is it not there already in the *kenosis* – as the New Testament would call it[17] – the readiness to forego one's own, in order to delegate which is evident in the entrustment of the created order, in part, to human 'caliphate'? In another way, any recruitment of the human into divine employ, as in prophetic apostolate, means that 'almightiness' stoops to dignify the human agency. In the case of the Qur'an this – Islam holds – has happened in the most hallowed and crucial of all realms, that of bearer of divine words as being the mouthpiece of the Eternal, the surpassing office it greets in Muhammad.

Perhaps fitting any 'measure' or 'clue' to the meaning of Allah as *akbar* is unnecessary, if the sum reality is fulfilled in *Shari'ah*, if – as one writer has it – 'the aim of the Qur'an is man and his behaviour, not God'.[18] The core of theology would not then need to be in any way conceptual, with words like *akbar* not denotative but merely audible and usable. But even then, in this strictly pragmatic view of 'revelation', its psychic currency, its social rule, would surely still assume some 'characterization', if that law was ever to be definable as 'good', 'just' or 'beneficent'. Even so rigorously legal and formal a version of 'Holy Writ' as concerned with obedience more than worship, must still pre-suppose an imagination to bring those descriptives of law into human cognisance. Centuries of the

Sufi tradition of meditation on 'The Names of Allah' (*Al-Asma' al-husna*) would rebel against a 'Lawgiver' somehow neutrally above the Law He gave. So also would the using of those Names themselves in the art of *dhikr*, as 'recollection of God', borrowing, however mysteriously, what was humanly referable to the divine nature.

That element in the currency of the 'Names of Allah' is borne out by how the meaning of *akbar* comes into reference by the command of Surah 17.111; *kabbirhu takbiran*, 'Magnify Him with all you know how.'[19] The Arabic construction summons absolutely into employ all the human powers of adoration and 'esteem'. Hence the centrality of *takbir* as the heart of Muslim piety.

The reach of *akbar*, if a salient example, is only one instance of the 'writ of readers' in the interior business of theological vocabulary. That business has not been eased by the reluctance, to which the Muslim mind is often prone, to engage with its demands. The naïve formula: 'It means what it means' is either too simple or too dangerous. If there is diffidence about concepts, there is poverty in eluding them. Take that 'piety' word some lines back. What exactly are *taqwa* and *al-mu'ttaqun* and other derivatives? Having to do with 'the fear of God', the 'awe of right godliness', and the 'protection' that overshadows it can also extend to 'be wary of' or 'ensure against', or even 'obviate a danger'. Could such wariness in a fearing sense of God, in doing or refraining from an action, constitute such regard (for this or that) 'out of fear of God' as ever to come close, positively, to the love of neighbour out of love to God.

Placing *taqwa* as the very essence of Islam, Fazlur Rahman also relates it squarely to the central Biblical/Quranic theme of 'human caliphate', when he writes:

> The best way to define *taqwa* is to say that, whereas action belongs to man, real and effective judgement upon that action . . . lie outside of him.

Hence, via *taqwa*, the intimate correlation between human liability and the moral 'education', via guidance, reminder, warning, which the Qur'an affords. Awareness of impending divine 'reference' of all things in judgement

> can be effectively conveyed by the term 'conscience' if the object of conscience transcends it . . . It is proper to say that 'conscience' is truly as central to Islam as love is to Christianity.

'*Taqwa* . . . means to be squarely anchored within the moral tensions, the limits of God.'[20] *Taqwa* – we might say – is living under 'holy writ' in deep emotional tune and active harmony with its authority.

Akbar and *taqwa*, crucial as they are, serve to exemplify the steady vocabulary duty of 'the writ of readership' in the Qur'an. There have been useful compendia of New Testament words, their nuances and associations, the study of synonyms and the incidence of terms in contexts. There is need for a similar 'dictionary' of Quranic vocabulary, not to explore its allegedly foreign to Arabic instances,[21] but to savour from a literary as well as theological angle the import of its salient terms, the latent secrets of its eloquence. This must be urgent, not only to redeem and illustrate the emphasis on 'matchless Arabic', but also to implement the Qur'an's own rubric in Surah 3.7 as to terms 'categorical' and 'allusive' or 'allegorical'. From one angle, being 'holy writ' is 'categorical' even when obviously figurative, but only so provided that the hidden associations of words in their extra-Quranic usage are fully appreciated.

These literary duties, however, are only part of that intellectual intercourse earlier noted between 'historian' and 'theologian' in the care of readership in 'holy writ'. The history of words belongs with how they avail for scriptural conveyance of faith. History itself, though, figures still more taxingly in how transcendent meanings, divine truth, can interweave with empirical events and earthly story.

This question has been implicit in all the foregoing. It requires in the chapter that follows to be squarely raised and sifted.

Chapter 7

The Time and Place Factor

I

IT WAS STATED AT THE OUTSET THAT Islam and Christianity are faiths that believe in the significance of history. Bible and Qur'an alike have that 'certain sympathy' which perceives a created order given, as a divine/human project, into the responsive and responsible care of humankind on the part of One who has not done so 'in jest' or as 'toying with a plaything'.

This means that they are Scriptures deeply committed to the 'time and place' of history. The Biblical tradition stands in the revelatory incidence of 'chosen history', from Exodus to Exile, via 'covenant' and 'land' and 'peoplehood' vested in their inter-action with these factors in their own formation. The Christian faith identifies the decisive history in the living personality of 'the Christ of God', known and loved as 'the Word made flesh' at the defining instance of the Lord who so willed to 'dwell among us' in His disclosure of 'truth through personhood'. Both these dimensions of the Bible take on the documentary form of scriptured text understood as presenting dependably the words and deeds, the course and character, of their immersion in the fabric of the story.

Differently, Islam with the Qur'an its credential, understands the direct mediation of a divine text, which – over a brief period of years and through the course of a single prophetic *Sirah*[1] – accumulates into Allah's ordained monitor of a responsive and responsible humankind, who by *taqwa* will find their 'conscience' in and through it. This text as 'Book', however, belongs with event and locale no less inevitably – if in contrasted sequence to the Biblical situation – than the other faiths. The Muslim Qur'an is 'the Book of God' by its mediation as 'Word made language', so that, unlike the New Testament, it is not the textual token of a revelation more ultimate than itself but the very text of that revelation as ultimate.

That distinctive feature of which perhaps there were intimations in the

79

Hebraic world,[2] entails the Qur'an equally in the 'where' and 'when', even though the 'how' of becoming Scripture is in contrast. It is in this their being essential – or merely incidental – to temporal and local situation that the Bible and the Qur'an are apt for a 'certain sympathy'. It is, in either case, a condition making great demands on the aptitude of their readership, whose tests are not simply those of language and vocabulary reviewed in the preceding chapter but now of how 'the once there and then and thus' abides as 'the final here and now and ever' of the lapsing centuries into the riddles of our own.

II

Circumstance in the incidence of the Qur'an is familiar enough – Surahs identified for Meccan and Medinan, events between those two cities and around them, the watershed of time-transit between them, the locale of the Hijaz and the coastal littoral on the eastern shore of the Red Sea and the hills inland, the tribal society of the seventh century, the medium of the Arabic tongue in its supreme eloquence at that point in its story. All these reflect themselves in the fabric of the text, its idioms, its parables, its whole character. The Qur'an's received 'eternal dimension' does not escape the incidentals of a temporal, territorial scene. Rather the one recruits these in the context of the other.

More specific events in the sequence of the Prophet's *Sirah*, coinciding so closely with the *Tanzil* of the Book, provide what classic commentary has long called: *Asbab al-nuzul*, 'the occasions' of the mediation of the text. They serve to clarify as *in situ* what the sequences are *in via*, the settings by which the text is to be understood.[3] It would be wrong to think them the 'causes' of the revelations, for these are pre-existent in the Book's eternity as faith understands. Yet they constitute the points for its intelligible interpretation – in that inescapable role we saw earlier of a 'Book's People' in their readership.

Thus it was integral to the Qur'an's nature and to its doctrine of itself that it should incorporate time and place. If it were to be earth-seeking, human-relating, it could not be otherwise. Clearly, therefore, the idea of *Asbab al-nuzul* prompts the further question: Why this Arabia, why this seventh century, why these twin cities with their immediacies of tribe and trade, of distance from the great centres of imperial power? The question only presses because this 'there and then and thus' text intends 'all worlds in mercy' and a finality by which it must belong everywhere. If the immediate local context was vital to a text's interpretation, by the same logic the ongoing context of contemporary readership must serve to elicit the meaning of its durability. Datedness is a loaded term in the use of those who blandly equate the more recent with the more wise. Yet it applies as the necessary corollary of any historical revelation rooted in particular culture, language, and locale. Doubtless the art of inter-associating the first 'where/when' and the present 'here/now' will be a difficult duty making responsible demands, but it may not be foregone if texts are not to become virtual museums of bye-gone lore.

It is evident that Biblical studies have long been pre-occupied with the time-setting of Hosea or Jeremiah, the significance for Isaiah's inaugural vision of 'the year that King Uzziah died', or with the ethos of Galilee and the movements of first century Judaism during the ministry of Jesus and thereafter. It is not merely that the modern urban world rarely muses on shepherds and sheep, so that all the pastoral imagery of Gospels and Letters alike seems to it archaic. It is, more, that intelligent readerships of whatever Scripture have to reckon with how a historical particular yields an inclusive transcendence, whether it be in terms of a divine personhood or of a heavenly script being a humanly legible document.

Given a divine purpose in the incidence, the question follows as to the point of its timing. 'Not one but all mankind's epitome' – as a poet wrote in another context [4] – has to be the sum, whether of Yahweh in the destiny of Israel His people, or of 'God in Christ', or of Allah's sending of the Qur'an, if these events-in-time – with their faith-interpretation drawn from them – are to be each the vehicle of learning and living the human mystery. To be 'final' is to be where truth, devising a situation, has given to ultimate meaning a habitation and a home. Only so has a stretch of history focused the eternal.[5] It would seem reasonable that any mind, external to all – or all but their own – claimants to finality, should be free to assess them gently by how realistically they interpret human experience, how adequately they sift and sanctify it. To belong, from first defining time to current demanding time and duly appreciating their difference, is surely the honest task not merely of survival presence but of contemporary relevance.

At once, in facing that task a variety of questions arise. Are Scriptures within themselves subject to internal revision by their own evidences? That apart, are there hidden, latent meanings that will only come to light in the passage of time? If so, by what authority are they recognised and validated? Can texts come to mean what their authors never intended or could never have foreseen? Or, in the case of the Qur'an's *wahy*, might it have potential reading alerted by the will, devout or daring, to think inventively in altered place and time?

There have been diverse answers and initiatives by trustees of Bible and Qur'an alike to these questions. The Hebrew Bible has been revisingly read by the Oral Torah and in midrash of the Talmud. We learn of Moses, sitting with the Rabbis, consenting to be over-ruled by them as to what his Pentateuch meant. The Book of Ruth would seem to be over-riding the sharp exclusion of 'the alien' commanded in Leviticus and pursued by

81

Nehemiah.[6] Hosea would seem to be re-ordering the familiar interpretation of the Exodus as eternally designating 'the people of God' under their Yahweh.[7] Jeremiah (31:31) tells of 'a new covenant' and bequeaths a phrase which becomes the title of the Christian Scripture.

Jesus in the Gospels revises what was 'heard said in the old time' with his bold 'but I say to you', replacing 'the yoke' of long sacred tradition, authority-laden, with the 'yoke' of a gentler 'learning' (Matthew 11:29–30). The innovative 'Gentile inclusion' in 'new covenant' chartered in the Acts radically revises the origins out of which alone it could have come. Then the 'Gentile' offering for Jerusalem gives a new quality to the spiritual debt owed by them to 'the mother city' as a new quality of practical ministry in reverse. In sundry other ways the Bible proves eminently revisable within itself, extending – if also straining – the logic of its own unity.

In the case of the Qur'an, Muslims have had, since the Qur'an itself, the plain warrant of *naskh* or 'abrogation', whereby a *nasikh* changes its *mansukh*.[8] The scholars have long discussed its application and often sought to limit its arguable range. In respect of particular legal provisions or prohibitions, its application is simpler than if effort is made to invoke it in respect of non-legal matters.

The 'abrogation' theme is clearly consonant with the logic behind *Asbab al-nuzul*, 'occasions' being so crucially the clues to significance. The task is harder if we ponder why Surahs (all save Surah 9) are so carefully denominated Meccan or Medinan. For much in the contents of these Surahs is in tension with the other.[9] Does that decisive divide, under-lined by the dating of the Islamic Calendar as 'the years of the Hijrah', suggest there was a *de facto* 'abrogation' – though never explicitly stated – between the two 'eras' of the one *Sirah*? The rubric through the Meccan period to the Prophet was: 'Your sole liability is the word given you: Upon Us (Allah) is the reckoning.' After the Hijrah that singular 'preaching' continued but was then corroborated by the emerging legitimation of the use of force in response to what was perceived as the hostile intentions of the Quraish. Those perceptions from the still precarious tenure in Medina were realist enough and that rejection still remained the posture of their enmity, an enmity all the more persistent now Muhammad was at large, no longer under their duress.

Even so, by other lights than those which then obtained, and were still rooted in the *balagh* rubric, a patient education of the Yathribites and others into the Islam which had now entrusted itself to their mercies might have gently left Allah's 'reckoning' with Allah alone. Instead, it was taken as entrusted into the hands of 'emigrants and aiders' alike to implement in terms of conflict joined. Its joining was steadily more authorised in the ongoing text of the Qur'an in its Medinan *tanzil*, until 'death dealing' (*qatl*) was a 'lesser evil' than *fitnah* (active subversion of Islam).

Traditional Islam has always assumed that this *de facto* 'abrogation' of the founding Meccan precept was also *de jure*. The Qur'an gives it no reason to think otherwise. On the contrary, it explicitly rules it valid. Yet, given that *naskh* on Allah's part is 'by something better' (Surah 2.106), and given things earlier considered about conscience, the moral question would still hold, as to whether Islam was a religiously truer thing in its Meccan word than in its Medinan wars. That moral issue would, of course, depend on criteria of religion and of ethics and also on the reading of local and temporal exigencies.

Beyond these, however, and more importantly, *naskh* or no-*naskh* in this theme astride the Hijrah, there is the burden of what finality-Quranic yields for the guidance of today? In the global scene we have yet to examine in this chapter, ought religions to continue to be enmity-shaping, enmity-practising identities, in a world yearning for global human community – a world which already has enough divisive factors in race, nationalism, profit, culture and suspicion obstructing peace? Is it not in the very genius of religion, in its referability to the transcendent, to discipline and curb these elements of strife, rather than fuelling and fanning their fires?

These questions are urgent because there are many in the modern world, across all continents, who fear that religions are incorrigibly the breeders of hate, the purveyors of insanity, whose banishment from the human scene is devoutly to be desired and pursued. Since that conclusion is really asking for religion more duly 'religious' in conscience, tolerance, patience, hope and humility, its very vehemence, the vehemence of despair, has to bring home how radically fraught our creaturehood has become, no longer now with the first Abraham, the founding Moses, the first-century Church, the medieval norms, the Meccan/Medinan transit, the bye-gone Hijri centuries. It is the 15th where we now belong by the Islamic calendar.

In recent decades the obvious question has been raised about the evident 'abrogation' (at least in emphasis and quality) of the Meccan Islam by the Medinan Islam, in that radical shift in the means of 'commendation' and of 'persuading' the obdurate. The suggestion of a few pioneers, mindful of where and when we now are, is that Muslims might wonder about 'abrogation in reverse', so that the Meccan version of a self-explaining, preaching faith now takes priority over the Medinan version of a self-deploying, fighting faith. It is a direction *naskh* has never proposed before, based on the sense that the really worthy *nasikh* is Islam's 'word' and the proper *mansukh* its armed, belligerent self which saw political power as its due asset. It is, however, a direction clearly more alert to the hope and sanity of the contemporary world.

It is important here to realise that the claim to finality works both ways. It not only assumes faith must be abreast of time in desperate flux but that this is no betrayal of what has been found 'final' earlier. A new 'here/now' does not thereby disqualify an old 'there/then'. The case for 'abrogation in reverse' need not, does not, disavow what – when 'once' was – was final at its 'then' point. The Medinan dimension abides in the fabric of the Qur'an just as do passages in the Bible which are now in virtual abrogation. It is daily recited and renewed in calligraphy. It will always belong, but as what held sway *then*. It had *ad hoc* warrant in its time-locale and was vindicated by how its skilled pursuit brought Quraishi paganism into the acceptance of Islam. Adherence may have been dubious or partial but these were matters capable of later handling and, meanwhile, 'great and manifest victory' had been assured.

Meccan priority only abrogates that scenario *now*, for the reason that 15th/21st century Islam no longer battles with an obduracy of that old Quraishi order, nor in a territory where it might thankfully provide an end to tribal feuding and mere 'gaps' of truce. It battles with more sophisticated superstitions, with global tensions and massive moral problems of poverty which are not for its single-handed overthrow nor apt for power alone.[10]

Were Islam in the present century to operate entirely in its seventh century Medinan terms, it would be inherently subversive of any régime it did not yet control or it would demand unilateral dominance wherever it was empowered. That might come to be partially mitigated by the concept of *dhimmi* status – allowing other faiths to be, as it were, 'Meccan' – on the condition that these could never be power-politically significant in any form. Rather their purely 'religious' existence would have pledged all such right away. This Medinan logic, of which there are painful exemplars still, is manifestly no prescript for the viability of world peace or the constructive co-existence of cultures. Happily in some measure Islam lives its Meccan self *de facto*, mostly in diaspora. Is that first self not germane to its true health and the benediction of humankind at large? That case and the hope it enshrines are the more cogent when we take stock of how apposite to it is the thrust of the *balagh* itself.

III

When the Qur'an has Allah affirming: 'We are not among the superseded'[11] the Scripture, too, is abreast of all the flux of time, the incidence of place. There is no need to find this ongoing relevance in naïve or merely inventive detection of its supposed prescience. For its 'abreastness' of new times is secure in the themes here explored in chapters 1 to 5. The spurious inventive sort needs to be noted only to be the more soundly deplored. To find that the Qur'an had anticipated the cutting of the Suez Canal, or the invention of photography or the deployment of X-ray technique, was to misread the truly religious intention of the Scripture. Nor could it intelligently add anything to the stature of the Qur'an's valid prestige already beyond doubt in its essential quality as *dhikr* and *huda* and *irshad* to humankind, their mentor in the knowledge and practice of *Islam* as the paradigm of true human *fitrah*, or 'right being'. If it was desired by pseudo-scientific claims to indicate how 'abreast' the Qur'an was, this was to locate its relevance by the wrong lights and to ignore the immediacies of *asbab al-nuzul*.

These ventures of ingenuity in bizarre 'readings into' the purport of the Qur'an were effectively disavowed and scouted by Muhammad Kamil Husain in his *Miscellany*. Thus falsely to appear to make good the Scripture's innocence of twentieth-century sciences brought its devisers no credit. Nor did it rescue the text from the implied discredit, seeing that the Qur'an's abidingness belonged elsewhere in spiritual witness and its moral demand.[12]

Perhaps more subtle but no less superfluous was the idea, often linked with the thought of Muhammad Iqbal, that the Qur'an was secretly aware of the nineteenth-century concept of evolution and 'natural selection.'[13] The deeply Semitic term *Al-Rabb*, 'the Lord' as a synonym for 'Allah', could be linked with the verbs *raba* and *rabba* 'to grow/increase' and 'to cause to grow' or 'to breed'. Allah could then be understood as 'the Proprietor' by whose 'rearing' all life and things had been evolved. 'Evolution' as a process could be aligned with creation as the purposive intention achieving through it.[14]

These and other case-makings, meant to underscore how time-wise Scriptures are, have in part been duplicated in respect of the Hebrew Bible, much more involved as that is in large other scientific issues – archaeology, biology and paleontology, by virtue of its vaster spread of centuries. The point, surely, in either case, is to appreciate 'holy writ' for what it purports to be and neither to tax it nor vex it with dimensions, whether of lack or of foresight, it does not possess. Thus to forego ingenuity is the better to enforce its inherent 'up-to-date-ness'.

There are two realms where, supremely – both in Bible and Qur'an – that abiding ripeness belongs, namely the 'caliphate' of all humankind and its distortion into idolatry.[15]

IV

How steadily more authentic, in awesomeness if not in principle, has that Biblical/Quranic *khaliqah/khalifah* perception of us humans become! The theme of a creaturehood in genuine entrustment seems more and more vindicated, both in its age-long incidence and its current degree. Contemporary technology pursues and enlarges its range with ever more relentless accumulation of techniques, ever more efficient manipulation of natural processes and the competences these afford because they are manageable and we are managerial.

That the entrustment is a genuine 'over-to-you' empowerment is proven in the very negligibility of divine reference in so much of the contemporary scene. 'Be and develop' is in no way withdrawn because we assume it in utterly secular terms. In the presence of the sheer generosity of our situation, we are blandly atheist and find no liberties withheld. Our licence is not conditional on our register of its trust-character in duly Scriptural terms. Was this the point in Jesus' parable and its reference to 'a far country' as being where we could opine the ever intimate Lord had withdrawn, only the more to underline the dignity, the independence His strange discretion had bestowed? Natural processes and our scientific enlistment of them do not discriminate between *kufr* and *shukr*, the graceless or the grateful, in their management.

This 'never-withdrawn-ness' of the human caliphate is only the more evident in how cumulative through the centuries the thrust of attainings has been, with generations of technicians enabling their successors and the whole subject to no retrogressive disinvention, so that time itself proves to have been – and to continue – a tuition in its own secret as a theological school of human practitioning. We learn the technical lessons well enough but how and why they are our caliphate less readily.

Yet from this unremitting forwardness of the sciences and the techniques and powers they yield us, the tokens of its quality as liable become more and more insistent. We have the techniques to make all humankind a single media audience yet grope for how to realise a global unison of sanity or to defeat the menace of terrestrial doom. The capacity for mutual self-destruction confirms that, in being entrusted with our planet in the 'caliphal' terms of science and industry, we are thereby entrusted with 'the all-of-us which is our world' in the 'caliphal' terms of society and law. They are one *imperium*.

Could there be any reading (call it 'myth' if you will) of the human situation as we find it than this of a divinely meant design of a human 'response' to 'responsibility' vested, so generously, so critically, in our capacity to undertake its privilege as a sacrament with God, no less than we operate it as a competence among ourselves?

It is just here that the second point in the 21st/15th centuries' relevance of the 'certain Biblical/Quranic sympathy' confronts us from their remoter time and place. The *imperium* which we are summoned to accept as sacrament with God we may no less usurp as an idolatry to ourselves. The Mosaic 'No other gods but Me,' the Quranic 'There is none but Allah', are not outmoded warnings for raw Israelis or pagan minded Quraish. They serve notice no less, and far more direly, on our contemporary scene where the 'having of false gods' is all too present a folly and a wrong.

Idolatry is far from being an ancient proneness in our souls. Even old Francis Bacon knew there were 'idols' of the market-place, and of the sciences and of the culture and of the nation.[16]

Indeed, there is something in the very liberty to be and to manipulate, to consume and to possess, that somehow invites to scepticism. That old 'Has God said?' whispers in the 'bosoms of men', breeding a basic suspicion about divine 'bad faith' arguing against any 'good faith' of ours. If the 'Be and possess' is materially unconditioned (apart from what in the earth-setting withholds intelligibility from intelligence) why is it said to be morally and spiritually conditioned? A far country Lordship can be successfully maligned, queried and at length disowned. 'This is the heir: come let us kill him and the inheritance will be ours.' The very character, the benign quality, of the empowerment have, by the same token, the capacity to be seduced. That is the corollary of their critical bestowal, the risk in their generosity.

And so it transpires that the tenant's tenure becomes all too darkly the usurper's province. Political power bends to become tyrannical. Money trades only to its own increase. 'A little brief authority' demands to have itself prolonged. Our temptation – and our capacity – to idolize our vested, or invested, interests are limitless and, all too often cavalier, with the warnings or the protests or the biddings that would curb them blandly ignored.

What is most sinister of all is that custodians of such warnings, protests and biddings, as mandate they have from 'the One Lord', may make an idol of their structure as the urgent native ground of these. Then, of all usurpers, the religious ones are the most heinous of all. Is this – so evident in history – the inner side of the general danger that to be entrusted is to grow trust-perverting? If custodians at large may grow unworthy, what of the custodians of custody, the religious mentors of humankind?

For these are uniquely tempted, 'serving the greater cause', to 'make the cause serve them', as monitors of the monitored. Then all the compromises of power, the violations of privilege, the distortions of authority that beset other realms of human action too subtly invade the precincts of religion.

Religions as themselves in some sense idolatrous may seem an uncongenial, indeed an impossible, notion to many in the business of religious self-esteem. Yet historically it has been all too evident a menace in their life. It takes several forms – all of them in measure trespassing on the *khilafah* in God's bestowal and the right of conscience and of decision it is given to exercise. Faiths usurp their 'caliphally' consistent role when they become pre-occupied with the power-nexus, or when they presume to constitute some direct theocracy, or if areas of faith transform into régimes of mental subjugation in bigoted or obscurantist versions of themselves. All these invade the personal trust of creaturehood Semitic faiths are committed to defend and guide.

Thanks to 'the territorial dimension of Judaism',[17] by virtue of the 'people/land/covenant' reading of Jewish humanity, what became the Davidic tradition was always latent, with its religio-political under-standing of sovereignty. Exile reduced the time-span of its exercise and, as interpreted by Jeremiah, gave it both landless viability and Messianic[18] hope. It was when the Maccabees and then the Zealots after them sought to realise that hope in martial terms of Jewish power that 'the cause' became idolatrous, only later to learn the integrity in power-forfeiture.

Islam moved into its own parallel to political zealotry when, post-Hijrah, it left behind the exclusively religious authority of its Meccan *balagh*. The fourth century Christian Church was drawn into a similar path via the decision of the Emperor to adopt the Christian communities for imperial purposes and they went along with his 'conversion' as somehow a destiny of which God had been the benefactor. Through all the eventuating scenario, however, of Roman and Carolingian Empires and Papal supremacy, and the sundry post-Reformation nation states, that Christendom somehow always retained a latent distinction between itself and the Christianity of its pristine, pre-Constantinian years of perse-cution and imperial distraint. This vital Christianity/Christendom distinction was long obscured and overlaid. It languished unsuspected and overborne through long centuries of near oblivion, submerged under the regnant legitimacy of the *status quo*. It needed succour from many sectaries and medieval or modern deviants, who sometimes themselves yearned to emulate its powered confidence. It needed succour also from nascent 'secularism' and the agnostic mind, deterred – if not appalled – by the intrusion of implicit compulsion in the realm of spiritual belief.

But it was always there, ready to commend its first definition of the genius of Christianity, as to the 'whosoever-will-*may*-come' nature of the Church's appeal and to the 'mind of Christ' in and beyond his Gethsemane. The present issue for Islam is that the partially comparable 'Constantinianism' of the Prophet of Islam in Medina is deep in the integrity of the entire faith. It is embedded in the fabric of a Scripture where it will always be read and inscribed and where its validity is never in doubt as ever enshrined. Even so, the Meccan singularity of *balagh*, of religious faith for its own sake and on its own merit, also persists undimmed and not to be erased, and the less fit to be ignored or relegated from the fact that the Hijrah itself – in no way a wild act of faithless brig-andage – was totally meant in the name of the Meccan 'word alone' and for its proper, or improper, sake.

So the logic has to be the plea of finality *and* its demand in the circum-stances of this twenty-first century when religions must, at all cost, attain to co-exist. For, otherwise, they exploit and deploy their political priori-ties in the pursuit of enmity-creating faction across the community of nations. Can there be for world-minded Muslims now this 'abrogation in reverse' which believes that Allah 'brings something better' – better by reference to 'where', and 'what' His world now is, but does so out of what was first disclosed in the *Tahannuth* of Mount Hira' and given a tongue in the suqs of Mecca?

But wait. Is not power indispensable to the well-being of society? Can the social, the civil, the cultural subsist without the political? Is not the international community, so-called, a polity of 'United Nations'? Can it currently be otherwise? Are not all these 'nations' in some measure both foci of power and habitats of religious beliefs often integrally related to their very identity? Was not Medinan Islam entirely right in believing that religious faith, far from abandoning the city state (which its Hijrah never meant to do) must be totally committed to it and in command of it? How can an honest religious faith abnegate the political order and leave it to chaos or contention and every kind of aberration? Were there not minds in the early Church looking fondly towards what Constantine achieved?[19]

The questions deserve respect. But the twenty-first century world is urgent for some measure of trans-national community, some degree of common peace-ensuring inter-liability of humankind. This cannot happen as long as the absolutist passions of religions continue to foment the confrontations of peoples, or dark absolutes of Zionism abet the irreconcilability of Israel to Arab neighbourhood, or the absolutes of militant Islam take over the mind of Palestinianism to submerge its other will,[20] or the hardness of northern Nigerian States disrupts the commonalty of a Nigerian nation, or the Al-Qaʿidah version of Islam plots to eliminate the West, or the West ever again conceives its world-relation in belligerently religious terms.

The 'religious' vocation in all these is to find the humility which alone commends their meaning. There is a deep distinction between being 'dominant' for long historical reasons, and being 'domineering' in intolerant terms. The former, where it obtains, will be a cultural destiny but one that leaves minorities viable, free and articulate. The latter can only embitter the scene, darken the earth and jeopardise the global future. Both will have more and more to engage with that 'disbelieving in belief' which belongs so deeply with technologised society and current dismay and disgust about religions at large. In that encounter those that only 'domineer' will never discharge their civil liability nor commend the soul that is in them.

We have arrived at the question mooted earlier, namely whether, within 'the writ of readers', Scriptures may possess and truly yield meanings not initially, or for long centuries, perceived by their traditional readers. Is there a prescience in them, not of the artificial order earlier noted and dismissed, but of a duly pregnant kind? In secular quarters, mainly in the West, there is growing interest in – indeed philosophies about – the crucial role of 'readership' in the fate of texts.[21] Some faith-people may consider 'holy writ' exempt from and exalted above all such peril. Yet it belongs with the very nature of that textuality to which 'revelation' is entrusted in taking written form. Alike with the Bible and the Qur'an, we have seen already how far the very arrival in language was immersed in scenes, times, people and hazards implicit in human terms. Hud, Salih and Shuʿaib in the Qur'an 'spoke' to a time beyond the years of ʿAd and Thamud by 'seconding' what Muhammad would be saying to his Meccans and so enlarging on their relevance. Within the Bible also there is this significant projection of past lore into further perception, as when Hosea re-ponders his people's Exodus or Jeremiah re-reads the logic of Exile.

The New Testament holds that 'things' from Jesus his disciples could not 'bear now' would be told them by dint of the Holy Spirit and the fourth Evangelist. What Jesus meant in words would be the clearer only at length by what he lived in deed. Though the early Christian Creeds are not verbatim in the New Testament, its faith is that they are implicit there and duly read from it by an obeying Church – and necessarily only by that means.

But is there 'yet more light to break forth'? ʿAqaʾid in Islam,[22] Creeds in Christianity, and the communal closing of the Canons in either case, would seem to imply that the answer is NO! Yet since time does not halt, nor living faiths stagnate as 'still waters' but are ever only rightly one with the stresses of the world, Scriptures also have to come within the purview of their growth in relevance.

The argument now surely has to be that humankind has come into a terrestrial experience, alike of menace and promise, hitherto unknown. It is one where religions become, in the deepest sense irreligious, if they only create enmities, connive with faction, suppress enquiry or trade rejections. Where their Scriptures seem, or avail, to underwrite these 'irreligions' they must be read – as it were – against themselves by a holding prior and contemporary of the blessed measure in which they also denounce them and commend the contrary. This means no compromise of their essential witness because its essence will be responsibly located in these terms[23] – terms which will, rather, liberate its theme and content for what they now must mean. The care of Islam, as in Surah 17.21–39, for integrity, justice, compassion in society ('weigh with just scales') will be the more appropriately operative when its political auspices are not monopolistically Muslim, as if these were only safe in its hands and other humans not liable for their relevance. The distinctive Christian sense of the place of vicarious love in the economy of God will be the more evident when this faith itself is not leagued with power and thus immune from its own mandate.

It is often urged that the hatreds and passions bitterly afflicting human societies are *not* the work of religions but instead of political forces and cultural conflicts or even racial/language factors. The plea finds little credence in the secular mind-set as a facile exoneration of the real complicity faiths have in sustaining or worsening these tensions. The exoneration is too naïve. Faiths themselves have a duty to dispute it if only to be honest with themselves.

All this lays a steady obligation on the community of faith. In respect of both Scriptures, community has long been writing in the margins, the side-notes of the Bible, the *hawamish* of the Qur'an, where the perspectives of the faithful, no less than the elucidations of the scholar, are set to enter. For while the text has the margins, the margins also have the text. The primary power of the one moves by the secondary leave of the other and all is inside the *khilafah* of our world-entrustment over which the text must preside. For that *khilafah* in both our Scriptures was entrusted to our humanity at a point antecedent to *all* the religious structures purporting to educate us in its discharge. Nor has it ever been withdrawn, despite the evident human capacity to ignore or defy it, even long after the final text of that education, whichever it be, was made available for us.

If, then, religions, foregoing monopolies but not absconding from the liabilities of political power, bring themselves in terms of witness about God and *this* humankind, they will be more truly honouring and serving the 'caliphal' gift their hearers have. For, as God gave it, it was a gift they were to tell and teach, not coerce and disown, as all compulsive, forceful devices do. Their true concern must ever be with the set of human minds and the springs of human will, as these bear, for good or ill, on the ways and works of our 'caliphal' order – and disorder.

Doing so, they may well find that their heaviest task is in the economic sphere, and here the most urgent onus is in the economic workings of the West. While it is true that areas of world Islam are extremely wealthy – as in Malaysia, Brunei, the Gulf Emirates and Saudi Arabia, Muslims elsewhere, as in other Arab lands and Pakistan/India, are much poverty-laden. It is, however, the United States and Europe, via the IMF and the World Bank, that unduly shape the socio-economic patterns of the other world. They do so, most of all in the USA, by insisting on standards of living that jeopardize, retard or simply cancel any possibility of these being replicated outside their self-promoting perimeter. They do so by safeguarding their own productive and commercial levels to the detriment elsewhere of their own 'free market' capitalist principle of money for ever creating money. Expenditure in subsidy, say, per cattle-head, trebles the sort of one-dollar-a-day subsistence rate of fellow humans in lesser economies.

Moreover, this direct or indirect oppressiveness, caught as the global situation is in all kinds of cultural imponderables, is darkly served by calculated consumerism, conjured by advertising techniques fuelling the acquisitive fire of presumed well-being whereever it can be drawn this way, to the obscuring of the sweeter values of content, modesty, reticence and common hope.[24] The burden for genuine religion is how these, in a sort of counter-culture, can reverse the situation. It is also how belief, faith-wise or with other goodwill, can steer the world economies towards greater justice and away from endemic poverty-making, implicit in the very workings of prosperity.

This happens, to a degree, in the pressure in the West for 'ethical banking', where the investor is not making profit by means to which he can only be guiltily indifferent. There is something akin in Islamic banking where the *Shari'ah* prohibition of *riba'* (usury) is applied by ensuring that the loaning of funds for an enterprise must mean direct participation in it. No shares ought to be staked where the investor is simply 'making money' in staying only anonymously involved in the social, moral demerits of what his funds are doing. Though there have of late been notable developments and success in Islamic banking, there must be doubt whether ethical or *Shari'ah*-based banking can be remedial as long as 'the bias of this world' remains.[25] It is for Muslim economists, with their theologians, to assess how 'sanctifying' of the world's economies *Shari'ah* banking can currently be. Sadly, the good offices of 'ethical banking' in the West often look like a palliative against the back-drop of financings that ferociously protect employment levels, indulge in devastating arms-trading, subsidise distortion of global marketing, and the endless devices of urgent competition and the worship of profits.

That fear might suggest that a religious faith must work unilaterally to command and control the political order. That conclusion is much to the genius of Islam and its age-long post-Hijrah tradition. A belief-system is folly – or worse – if it does not seize and hold the political order. It is useless, as it were, to think to take the politics out of politics. Only fools would dream that dream.

Yet the way of power historically has never proved a panacea. What it can attain has never been more than a modicum of justice, righteousness and peace, with the ever present danger of over-reaching itself, whether in tyranny or the inherent conflicts it always generates within itself. History is replete with revolutions that, in the long event, only changed the name of evil.[26] When they are pursued in the name and by the aegis of religion, they in no way escape this fate of powered structures. The faith in them forfeits the vital role of a monitoring conscience – a role faith can only fulfill as the committed critic of the power realm. Far from that stance taking the politics out of politics, its independent conscience puts the ethics into politics the more, seeing that only so does politics 'ethicise' itself.[27]

At a tangent here there is, not least in the world of the West, the necessary engagement of the 'secular' mind in the trust of *khilafah*, since – as we have argued – the granting to us *khulafa'* of that *khilafah* preceded the disclosure of *any* apostolic revelation for its guidance.[28] Nor are the technological competences, nor the political liabilities of the human 'caliphate' withdrawn because humans choose to disavow or merely neglect those revelational Scriptures. The sciences with their techniques, states with their 'secularities', abide and abound. It would seem evident that the perpetuation of creaturehood-in-trust is the very fidelity of the Creator who told His angels to 'prostrate to Adam', in the assurance that in the whole enterprise 'He knew His own mind'.[28]

Such is the 'seriousness' of the humankind-in-being we noted at the outset. This chapter's attempt to reckon with 'the time and place factor' has to pass where that 'seriousness' comes most painfully into view in the dark issues of eschatology. There is no area where the sharpness and burden of the Qur'an are more marked than in its version of 'the last things' but the ethical urgency of what it sees at stake is continuous with all the foregoing in these pages.

Chapter 8

In the End – God

I

NOWHERE is 'a certain sympathy' of Biblical and Islamic scriptures more dubiously argued than in respect of their eschatologies.[1] Yet no area of their inter-study is more germane to the central thesis of these chapters as to the clear authority of the mutual theme of humankind in entrusted *khilafah* dominion of the earth. For – as we noted – the 'seriousness' of that theme and its accumulated history demand the ultimate reckoning, the judgement on its stakes. Law can never be consistently indifferent to its reception nor careless of its verdicts. Were death to close all accounts, it would seem that ethical significance would pass from mortal life and society. More than two centuries ago, Immanuel Kant held that 'immortality', with 'God' in care of it, were necessary 'postulates', with 'freedom', of his 'Practical Reason' and 'the moral law within'.

'In the end – God,' however, must be the safest formula for a scrupulous eschatology. For the issues are many and bewildering. The questions multiply. How will the final reckoning deal with private persons and the public order, seeing that guilt and innocence are not always fully privatised?[2] How will some 'grand assize' align with the incidence of personal 'passing time'? If there be some interval stretching between dying and judgement, how may it transpire? With what may it be filled? May there be occasion for 'amends', post-mortal penitence, a saner, humbler self-review, the law's suspending action? Or will the experience – if such it be – of time-expiry seem to usher final things forthwith?

The imagery of Surah 7.172 could see the whole sequence of humankind's multitudinous generations one simultaneous audience, capable of responding with one entire 'witness' to the divine Lordship in answer to: 'Am I not your Lord?' Since those generations can only be moral and law-answerable because they are successive, final judgement – somehow repeating the simultaneity – can only be also of long anticipation. How, then, endured?

Most searching of all – given this divinely 'serious' situation of human 'caliphate' and its great positive intent, not willed out of 'jesting' – it occurs, at least to some, to ask whether or not inexorable condemnation, still more a perennial 'hell' of despair, must not represent divine defeat? The problem for eschatologies, however scriptured, of the relation between the temporal and the eternal, is none other than that of the relation of the ethical to the divine. Perhaps this is where questions have to pass into reverent silence. For if, in the end, the religious call is uncompulsive, ever turning on option in the human will and heart, then there must be place for an obduracy, an unheeding that will not relent but wills to perpetuate itself. In that event, can some hell ever be 'unhelled'? Or if there be a divine love that is more resourceful, even those resources, going beyond law, will still, being those of love, be without duress, distraint or violence to freedom. Shall these then – over against human recalcitrance – be no better than a nobler failure? We have arrived at the supreme anguish of all eschatology, which maybe we could only escape by abandoning our Semitic loyalty and retreating to an Asian Buddhist view that resolves all by dissolving our illusion of liable selfhoods and serious global history.[3]

First paragraphs have embarked too far on a vista of conjecture. It is time to turn back to explore our actual Biblical/Quranic measures of things eschatological and their exegesis, without excluding difficult thoughts.

II

What is immediately paramount in the eschatological view of the Qur'an is its intense individuality and its personal loneliness. The non-Muslim reader finds a certain repulsion from the stark finality of eternal verdict for *muflihun* and the *khasirun*, the 'prospered' and the 'losers', and the stark perpetuation of the contrasted conditions as, whether for good or ill, an inexorable destiny, *innahum khaliduna fihi*, 'eternal dwellers' whether it be 'the Garden' or 'the Fire'. There are accents of the same 'inexorable' in the Biblical world but always somehow tempered, as we must explore, by the Messianic dimension and by the New Testament sense of 'the Lamb in the midst of the Throne' and 'judgment' vested in the Christ of God.

'To return to Us is the destiny of each and all. Whoever has done good deeds, being a believer, will not find his endeavours denied. We ourselves are his recorder. Anathema is laid upon a community We have caused to perish ... Then there are the unbelievers, their eyes wild with terror saying: "Woe betide us, we were heedless of all this! We were evil people."' (Surah 21.93–95, 97)

'The trumpet is sounded: it is the Day of which dread warning was given. Each and every soul comes attended by an escort urging it on and by a witness. "You were negligent of this. But We have taken the wraps off you and now today your sight is keen." And one self within him shall say: "This was always with me as a reality."'

'Throw, throw into *Jahannam* every obdurate unbeliever, every one who impedes the good, transgresses and persists in doubt and who sets up another god alongside God: cast him to condign punishment.'

'His other self says: "Our Lord, it was not I who provoked him to sin: in his own waywardness he was far gone." The Lord said: "Do not remonstrate together in My very presence. I had already given you My sharp warning. There is no changing what I have spoken. I do My servants no wrongful thing." On that Day We will say to *Jahannam*: "Are you filled?" and it will respond: "Are there yet more to come?"'

'Into close proximity with the devout God-fearers the Garden will be brought, with the words: "Here is the reality of the promise made to you and to each and every penitent, careful in law-abiding, fearing the all merciful in the great unseen and coming with a contrite heart. Enter here, in peace: this is the Day of immortal life." There they have what they desire and with Us there is ever yet more.' (Surah 50.25–35)

That the mortal creature is in constant moral crisis is plain enough, with an insurrectionist self at odds with a conformist one. The ethical intention of the Qur'an seems to be to instil a law-abidingness by the stark depiction of the eternal consequences that wait upon it. The dire warning is meant as alerting each and all to an eternal 'either/or' with all the onus on a mortal here-and-now, 'forwarding' selfhood into an ultimate calculus from which there is then no escape. What is here serial and cumulative is then decreed as the fated evermore.

Two features obviously emerge when pondered alongside the Biblical scene. One is the Qur'an's realistic measures of sin as guilt-and-fate-laden, the deep heedlessness of wrong of which human *ghurur* proves capable, the utter self-deceptions to which we are liable. How might what is so dire from these in that 'Beyond' be turned to obviate their havoc in the here and now of social time and place? Ought not so grimly charged a future be brought to bear remedially, redemptively, correctively, on the living present, seeing that post-mortal reckonings so sharply tell the stakes it carries?

The question ties into the second aspect of Quranic eschatology. The individualism is so stark. One's personal members – lips, limbs, hands, feet – will all witness to their blame and reproach. The reckoning with our waywardness will have the witness of our own self-accusation, and there is no intercession.[4] The grand assize excludes all things vicarious – things so central to the New Testament's economy of the eternal. While, on the one hand, all that *ghurur*, that heinousness of wrong, was socially injurious, humanly destructive and done 'in despite of Allah' (as judgement eloquently tells) what, on the other hand, of its breaking out beyond any sharp personal monopoly into the social order, alike of humankind and under God?

For in that wider realm, it becomes clear that something of its significance is vicariously outside the personal sphere. The guilt is indeed inalienable, but the effects are extra-personal being always inter-personal. One man's wrong is another man's grief and woundedness. From such relatedness – human or divine – surely remission may come, via a taking-on of 'woundedness' that exacts no revenge and rises to forgivingness. Then, in some measure, there is – not exoneration – but an 'overcoming of the evil'. The question presses whether the divine *Rahmah* of *Al-Rahman al-Rahim* is of such an order, and in sublime terms.

The Qur'an's principle, however, in human relations seems adamant. *La taziru waziratun wizra ukhra*, 'No burden-bearer bears the burden of another' (Surahs 6.164, 17.15, 35.18, 39.7, 53.38). In respect of guilt this truth is incontestable. In respect of consequence, it cannot ever apply, seeing that what results from others' guilt bears heavily upon victims and preys on sufferers. There runs through all life and society, from the womb in birth to death in battle, the toll of 'burdening'.

Another cluster of words re-inforces this veto in the Qur'an on things vicarious. 'We – or Allah – do not charge any soul but for its own' (Surahs 6.152, 7.32, 23.62, 65.7, in the passive: Surah 2.233). The verb, as in the other 'weighing' verses, has to do with 'reckon' and 'measure'.[5]

In this context there is also the question, not only about the privacy of reproach but concerning the solidarity of guilt and – in the latter – the reality of collective sharing and, perhaps, therefore, a measure of implicated 'innocence', the entangledness of wrong and sin being so marked in human affairs. Situations that are overpoweringly social, inclusively collective, must not be seen ever to ignore – still less absolve – the private share, however minimal and probably unavoidable. But nor must they implicate and condemn, as if the operating factors had not been multiple, as in the crimes of racial prejudice, exploitation, oppression, tyranny and social bias – all the evils the Qur'an comprises under *zulm*. *Al-azlam al-ijtima'iyah*, 'the social wrong-doings', admit of no private exoneration but *zulm al-nafs* in them is only justly read in their public character.[6]

The lonely individuality of the Qur'an's eschatology is the more awesome from the horrendous descriptions of an erupting universe, with falling skies and exploding stars and elements melting in fire and heat. In these there are close resemblances with some of the dire Biblical prophets like Nahum and Zephaniah. Just as Yahweh or Allah sustain the physical world and the planets in their orbits, so ruptures of that created order in earthquakes, volcanoes, and dread features of cataclysm accompany the inauguration of 'the Hour' and 'the Last Day'.

On the one hand, as we saw earlier, nature's dependability tells the positive of divine intent:

> 'Here is no jesting message but a word that is absolutely critical, as sure as the return of heaven's rain and the answer of the fertile earth . . .' (86.11–14)

so the 'breaking of the nations,' and 'multitudes in the valley of decision' (Joel 3:11f.) are heralded by calamitous disaster shattering the once ordered world.

> 'By throes that overwhelm, by energies ever at work, by buoyances borne in space, by precursors passing already, by forces disposing what must be – on the Day when the blast convulses the earth and there follows a blast yet again, on that Day all hearts will be filled with agitation and all eyes with dread.' They ask: "Are we in truth to be restored to our former state though we have become wasted bones?" That, they say, would be a pointless recurrence. One single arresting cry – and there they are, stark awake!' (79.1–14)
> 'The Hour draws near: the moon is split in twain! (54.1)
> 'The imminent Hour striking! Ah! The dread striking! What can make you realise the imminent Hour striking? The Day when mankind will behave like bees swarming wildly and the mountains will swell like wool that is teased by the carder's hand.' (101.1–5)
> 'Indeed, they deny the Hour and for those who deny the Hour We have made ready al-Sa'ir. When al-Sa'ir sees them afar off, they hear its crackling and its roar. When fettered together they are thrown into a confined area within it, they pray to perish there and then. . . Cry not today to be made to perish once! Cry for many perishings!' (25.11–14)

Thunder, lightning and calamitous upheaval betokening divine wrath were familiar enough in the Biblical world, as in Psalm 18. Divine retribution, as in Amos 9, is seen as in league with the inescapable wrathfulness of elemental things, consonant with the anger of Yahweh.

In the over-all picture, however, the stark and lonely individualism of the Qur'an's 'end things',[7] with personal reckoning and retribution, come much later in the Biblical story. There, for long, the theme of judgement (always in any generation 'the last') is bound up with epic history. This was inevitable given the Hebraic setting of land and people, of covenant and election, intensifying any general *khilafah* into their own corporate destiny. Divine wrath was visited through the scourge of 'Gentile' powers being His instruments – to be themselves requited after their function was fulfilled. The theme of judgement is not, then, the private self, but the nation. There is historic vengeance in this world on the collective peoplehood, not – otherwise – their soul investigation. Only then, as in Jeremiah and an exilic Isaiah, does exile begin to compel 'searchings of the private heart' and the exploration of accountabilities essentially personal, as in the concept of a 'saving remnant' in face of a largely apostate nation.

Nature may indeed be convulsed in this cataclysmic turmoil but the real judgement is upon 'the wicked'. To be comprehensively destructive and nugatory is not within the divine purpose. Even in 'the valley of Achor' must be found 'a door of hope'.[8] It would seem fair to conclude that the Quranic personalism in respect of what 'saves' and what 'requites' stems, via this contrast with the Biblical, from the inclusiveness of its sense of *khilafah* as non race-exceptionalised anywhere, but inclusively enjoyed as the common privilege of all humankind and fit, therefore, to be examined in the personal unit of the self. By the same token, there is something wanting in its failure to embrace in judgement the inter-play of the singular and the plural in the human story and its ethical burdening toward 'the Day'. We have to turn back to the Qur'an's portrayal of its incidence which dire convulsions and disasters heralded.

III

It is important to distinguish between the Qur'an's depiction of the last things and the elaborations which developed in the course of Muslim Tradition.[9] The Qur'an is one with the saying: 'It is decreed for man once to die and after this the judgement' (Hebrews 9:27). For there is a *barzakh*, a 'bar' behind us in the incidence of death which stays any impulse to return, thus confirming the defining 'seriousness' of mortal years, the single span of apprenticeship into the due *islam*.

> 'Only when death comes to anyone of them will he say: "My Lord, send me back again to life: let me return. It may be that I will act rightfully where before I defaulted." On no account! That is mere talk on his part. For behind them there is a barrier in place until the Day of their resurrection.' (23.99–100)

What that 'until' means in terms of conscious experience stays the mystery it can only be. Later in the same Surah the dead are interrogated, rather, on how long that crucial tenancy of earth and time has lasted.

> 'He will say: "How many years have you lived on earth?" They will answer: "A day or perhaps part of a day. Ask those who have kept account." He will say: "Indeed you spent a brief time there – if only you had realised how brief." Did you really think that We had created you pointlessly and that you would not be returned to Us again?"' (23.112–15)

Impressions of brevity only intensify the truth of mortal crisis. The whole thrust of the Qur'an's eschatology is to have the acceptance of life the more vigilant, the more pre-emptively self-alert. It is as if we ought to live with a post-mortem imagination, on guard against the wiles and whims of every hour. Meanwhile

'When the trumpet is sounded on that Day there will be no ties of kinship among them and no asking help from one another. Those whose scales are heavy are the ones who will be in blessed state and those whose scales are light – their very souls are forfeit and in *Jahannam* will they abide eternally. The Fire will scorch their faces and livid will their appearance be. "Were Our revelations not recited to you?" the Lord will ask "and you treated them as lies?" "Our Lord," they will say "things went hard with us and that is why we lost our way in sin. Lord, bring us out from here: if we ever go back again to sin we will indeed be wicked men." He will say: "Away where you belong. Talk no more to Me."

Among My servants there was a group who said: "Our Lord, we have believed, forgive us then and have mercy on us, for You are the supremely merciful One." But those people you made a laughing-stock: your ridicule of them made you lose all mindfulness of Me, so bent were you on deriding them. This Day I have rewarded them for their patient attitude. They have come through victoriously."' (23.101–11)

Thus the verdict eternal is directly related to the Meccan preaching. The first hearers of Surah 23 were already ushered into the final scenario to which it belonged. Elsewhere the 'book' of deed-accounting is delivered, when heavy, into the right hand and when light into the left – the moment of utter anxiety, either of excess of joy or anguished despair. The former is learned eternally in 'the Garden', portrayed enchantingly in sundry passages.

'Then he who is given his record in the right hand will say: "Here read my book: it was in my thoughts that I would have to face my reckoning." His will be a blessed state in a celestial garden with clustered fruits ready to his hand: "Eat and drink to your heart's content as reward for all you did before now in days that are past."' (Surah 69.19–24)

Again the same note of mortal days – as it were – eternally minded about where they culminate.

'For those who truly fear God there is sure triumph, sheltered gardens and vineyards, buxom companions and a cup of overflowing delight. No idle talk will be heard there and no deceiving. Such is your Lord's recompense, a bounty and a reckoning from the Lord of the heavens and the earth and all within them, the all-merciful.' (Surah 78.31–37)

'But those to whom from Us the good reward already is given – they are far removed from thence (*Jahannam*). Not the least sound shall they hear (from where wailing is their lot), dwelling evermore in that which their souls desire. The awesome terror shall not grieve them. Angels will welcome them, "This is your Day – the Day you were promised, the Day when We roll up the heavens as the rolling up of the scroll for the records."' (Surah 21.101–4)

Nowhere are 'here and beyond', the mortal and the post-mortal, fused together so starkly as here in the Qurʾan where the ethic is the eschatology, the eschatology the ethic, set as they both are in the convulsive, dissolving, self-subverting *mise-en-scène* of nature's order, the very realm of this custodianship on trial – a trial strictly arraigning or vindicating its practitioners in terms exclusively of the Qurʾan's own incidence in and around its twin Arab cities. Islamic theology would sense a difficult, if not insoluble, problem around destinies from pre-Islam or of those whose alerting to eternity had been from other sources than this Arabic.

The analogy of 'scales' and 'balances' is one that comes readily to human minds. Ledgers have normal mention in the Qurʾan and the 'book' concept of their content instinctive to a scriptured religion. The imagery of 'right' and 'left', of hands dexterous or sinister, is well-nigh universal, and certainly familiar to the Biblical reader.

While never counter-partnering it, the Biblical picture only slowly moves in the direction of the Qurʾan's starkness of verdict – and, indeed, never reaches it. Turning as any such scenario must in any context, on personal resurrection in some bodily event, there was long – for Bible-makers – a perplexity about its possibility or rather a despairing scepticism. It was a dubiety of a different order from that of the pagans of Muhammad's world.[10] For centuries there was no clear theme of life after death in the Jewish mind, but instead a certain wistful wonderment born of the link between Yahweh and His people, and their covenant of the territorial. Might it be that individuals only 'survived' in the memory and the continuity of a landed and a 'chosen' people? In *sheʾol* ever cherishable souls were *rephaʾem*, 'shades', retaining – if at all – only a tenuous individuation.

Yet that 'cherishing' persisted as, majestically in Job 19:19–27, with 'apart from my flesh' claiming some 'vision of God'.[11] Or the psalmist (73:23–28) bold to see, or foresee, some 'being continually with Yahweh' and 'received in glory'.[12] Somehow, *Sheʾol* with its indeterminate blankness seemed incompatible with love between Yahweh and His people. Meanwhile, nation-wise, 'judgement' was happening in contemporary history by the machinations of heathen powers and the manoeuvres via them of the divine will.

As and when there developed, out of these perplexities or their ever deferring effect on hope, the theme somehow of a 'new covenant' or a renewed 'heaven and earth' (to be explored below), the share in these of the departed in *sheʾol* became the more urgent and, with it, the necessity of personal resurrection. In the Bible scene there were also the influences of Persia and the land and people of the Exile. Also as Hebraic minds became more aware of 'Gentiles' as fellow-humans some 'share of theirs in the world to come', if 'righteous', also weighed on Hebrew thinking. If, as theists, their minds shrank from any notion of divine 'defeat', or of 'success' only in the realm of 'the righteous and the Garden', personal survival or revival became crucial.

How long anyway was that span – in *she'ol* or where-ever – between demise and 'the Last Day,' how soon or how long would be the interlude between dying and 'the Blast' of 'the Trumpet'? The Qur'an, for its part, would seem to find them near simultaneous. If close relatives could be of no aid or succour the interval must needs be brief. Maybe the individual was faced at once with custodian angels conveying him/her to the Last Day. In any event, earthly time-sense would be no more.[13] If indeed the climax is immediate on demise its dire character would be the more stark. Or would it, seeing – for the Qur'an – crisis is all?

Meanwhile, as physical resurrection comes more into Biblical ken, we find aspects akin to those of the Quranic world, as to requital, 'where their worm dieth not and the fire is not quenched' (Mark 9:44, 46 and 48; cf. Jeremiah 21:12 and Amos 5:6 for parallel in historical time). This becomes the more evident the more it is realised that the nation, or even some godly remnant, is no longer the nucleus of penitence but rather the individual. In and beyond the Book of Daniel, in the apocalyptic writings and the Wisdom literature, there are sometimes tentative, sometimes bold, anticipations of how

'many that sleep in the dust of the earth shall awake, some to everlasting life and some to shame and everlasting contempt'. (Daniel 12:2)

David also has allusions to 'a book of life' and names therein set. This sense breathes on in the New Testament where, however, as reputed of the Sadducees, there were still the sceptics. It is, however, linked with perceptions of national 'Woes' and the prospect of national vindication, with the 'dispersed of Israel' restored, as in the late second century BC *Testament of the Twelve Patriarchs* and the Sibylline Oracles. New Testament eschatology, in its partial affinity with – and radical distinction from – the Qur'an is best explored after these national, or other, prospects of 'new earth and new Heavens'.

IV

With this personal equation, however, to which we must return, there has always been the haunting question of a 'hell' as final, irreversible and humanly soul-abandoning to eternal fatedness in the Qur'an's *Jahannam* as somehow a dereliction of the divine purpose in creation's enterprise with creaturehood and prophethood. It is the very intensity of its ethicism that demands such anxiety. As we have seen, and as the Qur'an reiterates, the experience of the 'damned' is of conscious 'heedlessness', of culpable neglect of truth during the 'once chance' realm of fleeting mortality.

> 'Some should say: "Alas for me! – things done and left undone before God and scoffer that I was," or someone should say: "If only God had guided me I would truly have been God-fearing," or should say at the sight of the retribution: "Would that I could go back a second time and be among those who lived rightly." But no! God would say: "My revelations came to you and you treated them as lies. You became arrogant and joined the ranks of unbelief."' (Surah 39.56–59)

There is something here akin to the parable of Lazarus in 'torment' (Luke 16:1–9) confining the vital regret to a 'too late' situation. In either case, though only apprehension or worse induces it, is it not in line with what needs – albeit mortally – to happen? Otherwise what is the point of the retribution? May it not be remedial? The very urgency of what is seen so stringently ethical in mortal life requires this 'why and to what end?' question about *Jahannam* and all else of its sort and significance. Yet the Qur'an, and some elements Biblical, cannot allow of anything remedial or purgatorial once private death has supervened.

Is it this apparent failure in the positive enterprise with humankind that prompts, with other factors also, the celebration of a 'new heaven and new earth' in the Book of the Revelation of John, closing the New Testament? Here hell itself is cast into 'the lake of fire' and 'there is no more sea' to parabolise those inaugural convulsions of doom and its Day. What can 'Behold I make all things new' (Revelation 21:5) mean when God dwells anew with a remade people and the I/we, the Thou/me, relationship is finally real and abiding? What might its secret be? What, even so, of the bliss/doom eternity elsewhere so surely scriptured? The moral imperative of the 'newness' is unimpeachable, but what of that past indicative?

Perhaps that question is only allowable to a Biblical theology. Yet it is noteworthy that the Qur'an also – if never suspecting divine 'failure' – nevertheless anticipates 'new creation'. The several allusions are enigmatic and would seem to be answering doubters about the possibility of corpses resurrected (cf. 13.5, 14.28, 29.20, 32.10, 34.7, 53.47 and 56.62), made credible in the clear light of a first creation and so 'No hard thing' with Allah, who was not 'exhausted by the first creation'.[14] There is always the renewing of the created order by dint of that procreation which is so clear a part of our human 'caliphate', as the Qur'an emphasizes.

There seems no escape from the singularity of the mortal world as our accounting house and of 'new creation' (as above) referring throughout

to post-mortal resurrection of persons accountable – except perhaps
Surah 14.19 which seems to be in that context. It runs:

> 'Have you (s.) not realised that God created the heavens and the earth in
> truth? If He so wills He will remove you (pl.) and bring into being a new
> creation – a proceeding presenting no difficulty for God!'

The immediate context is on familiar lines but what is that *bi-l-Haqq*,
'with truth'? And is the 'new mankind' the old resurrected?
Commentators find *bi-l-Haqq* to mean the fulfilment of its divine meaning
and purpose, potential as well as existent, so that its 'serious intent' is realized, lest otherwise it prove *batilan*, 'in vain', a possibility ruled out, for
example in 13.191 and 38.27.[15] This issue of not 'being futile' would have
to turn on what constitutes futility in worthily divine terms. Yet even if
our theology finds vindication of *bi-l-Haqq* in John's vision of 'new
heavens and new earth' where 'righteousness dwells' by 'God and man
co-dwelling' we still have the problem: Why never so in the old? Perhaps
in that dilemma the Qur'an's version is more honest and realist. Yet it is
the very intensity of its ethicism, making 'doom' so insistent and eternal,
that will not let the problem rest. Perhaps theology has to leave all in an
inscrutability inalienably God's.

Or we might first see what the New Testament's 'newness of life' might
mean. It derives from a different perception of how God relates to the
human crisis.

V

It might be fair broadly to express that different perception, as between
the two eschatologies and their source in God's sovereignty, by charac-
terising that of the Qur'an as the absorbing future of the present, and that
of the Bible as the saving present of the future, provided we learn the
Biblical in the full aftermath of the perceived reading of Jesus as the Christ
from which the Church derived its being.[16]

There is no doubt of the constant presence of Allah in the thought of
the Qur'an.[17] He is closer to humankind than any self's 'jugular vein'
(Surah 50.16) whence it follows that:

> 'Those who deny the truth of God and die in their unbelief, the curse of God
> and the angels and mankind at large remains on them – so abiding eternally.
> Retribution shall not be lightened for them and they will have no reprieve.'
> (2.161–62)

This 'closeness' of the divine, alike in the judgement of the waiting
future and the daily present, makes our mortality the arena where our
'forwardings' accumulate towards it. Allah is utterly 'near' as the great

assessor at the end of all we are and do. Among the most frequent of Quranic terms are 'Unto Him is our returning' and 'unto Him is our becoming', *Al-Ruj°a* and *Al-Masir*.[18] Both have the meaning of an eschatological logic pervading existence, a future destiny an ever present issue. This absorbing 'future of the present' is the more real by dint of the Qur'an's awareness of how often the departed deplore and bewail their 'negligence' (*ghaflah*) of it. Allah's presence is that of an impending moral reckoning in the justice of the 'scales', with mercy joined, but no post-mortal reprieve. Its ethic is its hallmark.

As for the Biblical 'present of the future', we have to await the mature Christology of the New Testament to have it in clear confidence, but its roots lie back in the old Hebraic sense of peoplehood, albeit now private, under the guardian care of their Yahweh. Judgement, as we have seen, was in the flux of current history – often at the hand of wayward heathen powers and demanding present repentance of that 'people' and so their territorial, or other, 'restoration' in a steadily moving encounter with what might chasten, refine and save them.

This in sequel gave rise to some ultimate divine 'salvation' in 'Messianic' hope of which the great prophets spoke and dreamed as their interpretation of divine fidelity – a fidelity bound into liability through current history. This Biblical sense of things became, in the event of Jesus and his ministry, the crucible of conviction concerning this 'Messianic' intent having been achieved by that ministry, conclusively read in New Testament faith as the 'incarnation' of 'the Word made flesh' and 'made perfect through suffering'.[19]

Ought we to conclude that this maturing faith, so evident in the Gospels and the Letters of the New Testament, absorbs and qualifies those aspects which, undoubtedly, echo more Quranic style retributions and condemnations where 'their worm dieth not'? At all events, there is this 'saving presence' here and now concerning the eternal future. Did not Jesus assure the penitent fellow-sufferer on Golgotha: 'Today . . . with me in paradise?' His original recognition of 'Messianic meaning', precisely where it was now recognisable, brought the eternal counterpart to pass for him.[20]

Throughout the Gospel narratives there was the perception of this 'kingdom of God' as both already present and yet to be awaited. It is 'among you' (Luke 17:21)[21] yet we are still to pray: 'Thy kingdom come . . .' (Matthew 6:10). There is a present reality about a future inheritance, where what it already contains will be consummated eternally and that 'eternity' will consist in its consummation. Is not this 'saving presence of the future' most articulate in the Johannine conclusion: 'Beloved, now are we the sons of God'? 'This is life eternal – to know Thee and Jesus Christ whom Thou hast sent' – 'We know that the Son of God is come and has given us an understanding to know Him that is true and we are in Him that is true . . . This is the true God and eternal life.' This assurance is captured in the confidence of that otherwise 'hard-labouring' mind in the Book of Revelation: 'His servants shall serve Him and they shall see His face.'[22]

To be sure, this vision or version of 'already ours' what is 'of the eternal' was partnered in New Testament writing by a narrow vista of *parousia*, the 'appearing' and 'return' of Messiah Jesus, and also by the repercussions of the Fall of Jerusalem, the loss of the Temple, and other pre-occupations of Hebraic heritage. As the *parousia* tarried, and finally resolved into a present possession of its meaning, Paul and others became concerned about those who (meanwhile) had 'fallen asleep'. They must certainly be gathered into the same 'eternal life', however faith might resolve that interlude which their demise inserted into what had been first understood as already possessed. Ultimately, with the non-*parousia* that problem would belong to all generations, yet their 'eternal life' would be theirs as the future dimension of their 'present possession'. Was there, or was there not, any place for intermediate purgatorial experience or were selves 'made perfect' in the vision of 'Mount Zion' in Hebrews (12:23) already so in earthbound terms?

Many tensions remain around this 'realised eschatology' and its bearing on other accents which seem Biblically discordant with it. It rests, however, on the central Biblical concept of divine 'engagement' in redemptive response to human 'negligence' – and more – of divine claim. We may not call it 'intervention' if thereby we imply some divine absence. It is rather a sustained solicitude about the human privilege-to-be, understood to take decisive shape in the Christology of the New Testament, its reading of Jesus and the Cross. This is the dimension the Qur'an excludes by incorporating the significance of Jesus wholly into the ethical education mediated by the 'messengers, and thus corroborating the Quranic 'future of the present' eschatology.

The New Testament's 'present of the future' in the here and now of eternal life, while not unanimous, seems confirmed by two other convictions it commends. The one has to do with 'all judgement assigned to the Son' (John 5:22).[23] It is 'the judgement seat of Christ,' according to Paul (Romans 14:10), 'before which we stand'. Being 'heirs of eternal life' does not exclude reckonings that belong but do not issue into eternal condemnation. Being by grace His 'sons and daughters' admits of no presumptions of immunity from accusation. Rather it serves to make a will to penitence perpetual, seeing that justification is never earned, or merited or worth-warranted, being ever 'this grace wherein we stand and rejoice in hope of the glory of God' (Romans 5:2).

Must not 'Christ as judge' mean that all verdicts are within the compass of the love that suffered, of Messianic fulfilment in the terms the Cross gave to it? If so, its very severity is a 'Go and sin no more', a deepening of *mea culpa* from the very depth of *mea gratia*. Does it not symbolise and transact how the divine 'ethical' is comprised into the divine 'redemptive', so that 'the gift of eternal life' is at once grace alone *and* honest with the selves we are and were?

The second conviction must be the New Testament vision of 'new heavens and a new earth', the 'making new' of humankind in Christ in the 'day of salvation' translated cosmically into the new habitation of God, whereby 'all things are made new'.

Eschatology, in any event, as noted earlier, can only be a realm of theological minding of the character of God. 'New heavens and new earth', ensuring in cosmic terms the finality of a 'new people of God', still leave us with the burden about the old and the inevitable 'failures of the grand design' in awesome part it knew, being itself assigned to end and be foregone in the new. Since grace and love are inherently uncoercive, we are still left also with the problematics of their failure in the case of the ever recalcitrant. There too lie deep issues around whether and how far the opportunity of answer had been realistic and, hence again, whether and how the option of faith might still avail in eternity about eternity.

Those who will to reach their eschatology – as they must in loyalty to all else in their theology, or their trust in revelation – see indeed 'puzzling reflections in a mirror'. And aside from the difficulties intrinsic to any eschatology, Muslim and Christian traditions of 'the last things' have been fascinated by how these might engage with history *per se*, as time and chronicle contain it. Both religions have elaborate versions of ultimate climaxes, the release of Gog and Magog as rampant powers of evil, the 'woes' of catastrophic story, the feats and defeats of *Al-Dajjal*, the 'antichrist' and the before-and-after of some 'millennial kingdom'. Muslim sources here were doubtless influenced by Christian conjectures and visions of the human future.[24] Disruptive or near ecstatic as some of these predictions have been, or only the stock in trade of excitement and anticipation, they still leave to sober theology, or more in the case of Islam to sober faith-interrogation, the divine disposition of all things under heaven.

VI

Yet, through them all, a final question remains – how should we understand those vivid images of the Qur'an and what resembles them elsewhere of tormenting fire, acrid smoke, bitter waters and, so desperately contrasted, the serene delights, the plentiful fruitage and the luscious verdure of celestial gardens? Given the ethical intent vested in either, they can hardly be imaginary. But can they be, in any perpetual persistence, duly ethical? Are they not only pointlessly vindictive and morally barren?

And will not the latter fail ethically of 'the vision of God' and resolve into a plethora of idle reward?[25] Are not despair on the one hand, or satiety on the other, their only consequence and, given nothing but their perpetuation, are they not themselves a reproach to heaven? How will they consort with the Qur'an's assurance that 'Allah has prescribed for Himself mercy', 'made mercy the charter of His will'? (Surah 6.54). How did 'mercy' rule or over-rule the verdict of the 'scales'? Only what theology perceives will yield an answer. Eschatology returns where all begins, to the divine will that we, as humankind, should have been so awesomely 'let be' in the critical privilege of the world.

Notes

Arabic translations and transliteration

Qur'an translation into English is from my *Readings in the Qur'an*, London, 1988; 2nd edition Brighton & Portland, 1999.

Arabic transliteration (the written when not the voiced) does not distinguish long syllables, nor light from heavy vowels. It notes only the glottal stop (medial as in Qur'an, final as in Karbala'). It has the final 'h' as in *Sirah* and *Qiblah* to avoid confusion where it does not occur, as in *ikraha* and *dhikra*. 'Quranic' is used without the glottal stop as – presumably – having passed into English, 'ic' not being an Arabic terminal.

Traditional spellings are used as in Mecca and Medina but it remains important not to be careless about words like 'Muhammad' and to avoid corruptions like 'Koran'.

The *ain* letter, initial, medial or final by ' distinguishable from the *hamza* '.

Preface and Precaution – Bible and Qur'an in Inter-Study

1   See: Robert Frost: *Complete Poems*, New York, 1949. The 'Lover's Quarrel' comes as the last line of 'Our Hold on the Planet' (p. 476), 'passing through the woods at evening' is on p. 275. Robert Frost (1874–1963) lived with frequent sorrow, his father dying when he was eleven, losing children in their infancy, a son dying in suicide, daughters suffering from dementia or depression and his own loves failing. He was led to ask (p. 493), 'If all the soul and body scars were not too much to pay for birth'? Yet the gentle lyricism of his farming scenes and images registered how 'sacramental' a mystery nature could be.

2   Echoing George Washington's word about what American foreign policy must never have (nor 'inveterate hatred') *vis-à-vis* any nation. It was his Farewell Address to Congress in 1796. See its application to US 'passionate attachment' to Israel since 1947/48 in G. W. and D. B. Ball, *The Passionate Attachment*, New York, 1992.

3   Assessing a passive co-existence this way does not ignore or disparage the efforts at intellectual discourse, from John of Damascus in the eighth century to Ibn Hazm in the eleventh and beyond. But, given the problematics in Arabic for the Greek of Christian Christology, these debates rarely reached

where they needed to come, in mutual comprehension or the recruitment of analogy and metaphor to overcome the failures of terminology. See further chapters.

4   In the much debated sense of Surah 2.143: 'We have made you as an *ummah* in the middle', 'a medial people, or nation'. Some take it to mean 'of the middle way' (in ethics), 'a morality that shuns extremes'. But it could well embrace this truth, so clear elsewhere, of a humanity mediating between heaven and earth, in achieving the will of the one in the affairs of the other. Some see the meaning as geographical, akin to the modern usage 'the Middle East'. See, further, Chapter 5, note 17.

5   The words Ernest Hemingway put in the mouth of his 'The Old Man and the Sea', speaking to the boy he took with him into the drama of his bout with the marlin. How aptly it fits our 'adventure' in the physical world.

6   As the novelist Iris Murdoch concedes in *The Sovereignty of Good*, London, 1979, about our being, categorically, 'on our own'. The view that 'Human life has no external point or *telos* is a view as difficult to argue as its opposite. I shall simply assert it' (p. 79).

7   It is clear that the Qur'an, as 'ethics' and 'eschatology' in one has both dimensions. See Chapter 8.

8   The *Shahadah* ('The sole reality of Allah as One' and 'Muhammad His Messenger'). The Arabic *Rasul-Allah* could never mean '*a* Messenger' but only 'the . . .' with the culminatory sense of finalising a sequence. The twin clauses (there is no 'and') contain creation and creaturehood as pre-supposed by the Unity of God *and* a realm of His sovereignty requiring the ministry of 'messengers'.

9   Surah 11.61: 'He brought you forth from the earth and made you colonists there.' *Istaʿmarakum fihi* uses the form which gave to modern Arabic the hated word *Istiʿ mar*, 'imperialism', or 'being established', *not* where we do not belong and usurp, but occupying by given leave.

10   A negative interrogative and therefore expecting the answer: 'Yes!' but awaiting it. This note in the Qur'an has to enter far into all our thought about 'omnipotence'. In context the whole assembled host of humankind – of all ensuing generations – is understood to have openly acknowledged that the true answer is: 'Yes!' See: *Am I not your Lord? Human Meaning in Divine Question*, London, 2002. See Chapter 5, note 10.

11   This theme of historical 'seriousness', of earth and humankind not being Allah's 'plaything', is plain in, for example, Surahs 21.16 and 44.38. It is confirmed in 38.27 where the word is *batilan*: 'We did not create the heaven and the earth and all between as a thing in vain (or futile).'

12   Here we need both senses of 'certain' – the proximate one (as in 'a certain man had two sons') because there are many who would minimise the idea or resent it altogether. Yet the point is altogether 'certain' in the complete sense. The congruity of Bible and Qur'an in this way is real enough (as will be argued later) to absorb or even nullify all other disparities that worried the old polemic.

13   The Gospel parable (Matthew 21:33–42, Mark 12:1–12, Luke 20:9–19) is very apposite here. For it bears out how the grant of fruit-liable tenancy can so readily develop into a bid for outright ownership by 'killing the heir' – the

ultimate logic in withholding the fruits. This 'human-inclusive' sense certainly holds – though the parable had implications meant also for the Jewish covenantal situation as the 'chosen' and 'landed' people. See Chapters 3 and 4.

14 For its own reasons Islam abjures the 'priest' word. Yet some 'consecratory' role is present in all sense or practice of gratitude in human life and in how we handle commodity. The umbrage among Muslims against 'priesthood' stems from its being an 'office' in liturgy. Since, however, it belongs with all and sundry in their privacy and public action, it only harnesses the sacramental principle all faiths have, whereby what we do tells what we mean, as in giving a kiss or having an embrace or offering flowers or prostrating the body.

15 See, for example, Raymond Tallis, *Newton's Sleep: Two Cultures and Kingdoms*, London, 1995, insisting that sciences are *not* unimaginative, nor the arts merely imaginary and, so, useless. 'What is true of mathematics – that it is at once a tool, a vision and a form of intellectual music – is true to a lesser degree of science as a whole' (p. 209). The arts and the sciences must be seen as complementary, either to the other.

16 Only by being so does it admit of any ethics, any human *khilafah* at all. Its being non-discriminatory as to whether we are 'secular' or 'sacredly aware' leaves that issue entirely in our hands. Without a religiously 'neutral' natural order, no 'religion' would be possible. In an odd way we have to realise that only occasion to be 'secular' makes possible the vocation to be *muslim*. The way nature was 'ordered' preceded any 'revelation'. Thus the question arises whether political power and statehood should not be 'neutral' as to religion, in the way that Allah's world is. If one faith takes over rule and government unilaterally, how do 'secular' folk retain the political aspects of their *khilafah* as that which Allah has not withdrawn from them?

17 Matthew 5:48. What follows is not the impossible 'Be ye therefore perfect' but *teleioi* 'inclusive' in this divine way. This does not mean that we keep no moral principles but that we respect the 'caliphates' of all, there being 'no coercion in religion' (Surah 2.255).

18 Surah 56.58, 63, 68 and 71, the last being 'the fire you strike out (with flints) and so kindle'. The sense of the verb in each case, *a fa ra'itum ma*, may have the literal sense of 'can you actually see . . . ?' But – more – the sense of 'what view do you have of . . . ?' This is in line with the Qur'an's frequent call to reflection, to *tadabbur* or 'intelligent appraisal'.

19 T. S. Eliot's 1921 poem, written in the weary aftermath of that First World War, has had a powerful impact on twentieth-century Arabic writing, perhaps – in part – because it shaped a mood of desolation around the Palestinian tragedy. See a personal example in Salah 'Abd al-Sabur, studied in my *Troubled by Truth, Studies in Inter-faith Concern*, Durham, 1992, pp. 166–86.

20 See note 15. The remedy is already there in the 'lessons' all science learns (and teaches) of honesty with evidence, humility to discard the obsolete, intuition to guess hopefully, diligence and patience in truth-pursuit. All of these are deeply religious 'virtues', and perhaps the sense of a 'ministry' that might equip compassion.

21 The *fitnah* term is right, namely a situation that examines not only what we think but what we are.

22 Ziya Gökalp (1875–1924), usually regarded as the mind behind the Atatürk 'reform', reduced Islam merely to the cultural dimension of 'being Turkish'. That identity was paramount, with any theological ethics or 'truth' absorbed into a culture of ethnicity. The story of twentieth-century Islam in Turkey in this context was well assessed in its near sequel by the Canadian scholar, Wilfred Cantwell Smith in his: *Islam in Modern History*, Princeton, 1957, 'Turkey: Islamic Reformation?', pp. 161–205.

23 Turning bizarrely on an alleged wrong transliteration of the Greek word *paracletos* ('the Holy Spirit the enabler') and *periclutos* – 'one praise-worthy', who could be Muhammad. The first word was there long before his seventh-century time. It could hardly have been misconstrued before he entered history. See this, and other items of wearisome polemic in: *Jesus and the Muslim*, London, 1985; Oxford, 1999.

24 'No compromise' in that we move from the 'status' of this or that 'Scripture' which may be left an open question (since it so far fails of solution) and we move entirely inside the 'content' – which is surely what any text invites us to do. Thus we 'acknowledge' them simply in terms of what we feel they would have us understand from them. It would be odd to think that the Qur'an (unlike certain Muslims) warned off all non-Muslims from its study. For when it began there were no Muslim hearers or readers. Its pagan audience still had to be won. Outsiders in either case need to defer to what insiders say of their own but not to the suppression of their own reading will and mind. For these the Qur'an itself is everywhere asking.

25 See note 6.

26 Perhaps this whole stance is captured in Surah 50.37: 'Surely there is point to ponder here for whoever has a heart or who heeds with alert perception.' The context is about the dark panorama of the human story.

27 Employing the Qur'an's term *qadar*, or 'measure' or 'evaluation' in a theological sense. See below Chapter 5, note 4 and Chapter 6, note 14.

Chapter 1   Divine Ends Set in Human Means – Creation and Cosmos

1 Perhaps we should only speak of a 'pause'. Certainly there is no *wa*, no 'and'. There is just the juxtaposition of the briefest theology and the most terse statement of prophethood. *Muhammadun Rasul-Allah* is a nominal sentence without 'is'. Cf. Preface and Precaution, note 5.

2 Pre-Islamic poetry is famous for its pathos, its laments over the costliness of blood feuding, child mortality and the inevitable forfeiture of all things mortal. Hence the sharp incredulity of the Quraish at Muhammad's message of 'corpses' brought back to life to face judgement.

3 Psalm 10:4. This chronic heedlessness is quite other than the sense of a 'lost-ness' about God which cries: 'O that I knew where I might find Him!' Such agonized will to 'seek and find' is the very intensity of a would-be 'heedful-ness'.

4 The phrase comes more than sixty times and *min duni-l-Rahman* in 43.45 and 67.20. 'The Allah we ignore' could well be the trade-mark of the pagan

Meccans, via a 'naming' that is not of Him exclusively (*shirk*) or via idolatry of every kind. The *Allah* word was not unknown (Muhammad's father was an ʿAbdallah) but it was not understood or used or meant as Islam required it to be.

5   The Arabic nominal sentence (note 1) makes its predicate one that must have the English *the*. To say 'Muhammad was a messenger' would require a different form of words. This singularity is confirmed in his being 'the seal' (*khatm*) of *nubuwwah*, 'prophethood'. Surah 33.40 'The Apostle of God is the sealing of the prophets.' Cf. Preface and Precaution, note 4.

6   For my part in *The Mind of the Qurʾan*, London, 1974; *The Privilege of Man*, London, 1968; and in the Introduction to *Readings in the Qurʾan*, London, 1988, Brighton, 1999. Among many Muslim writers Gai Eaton, *King of the Castle*, London, 1977 and Ali Issa Othman, *Islam and the Future of Mankind*, London, 1993.

7   The difference that point makes between *faʿ* and *qaf*. Some have conjectured whether the word in 2.30 might intend the other but the context is clearly about a 'deputyship', on the wanton conferring of which the angels complain as they already discern what the *khaliqah* is like.

8   The command *Usjudu li-Adam* . . . (2.34) uses the verb normally that for the worship of Allah, i.e. the 'prostration' in *Salat*. Thus it captures the fact that the angelic worship is not of the creature but in recognition of God's glory entrusted in His *khalifah*, the divine end invested in the human means.

9   For without nomenclature no knowledge can proceed (2.31).

10   Philip Larkin, *Collected Poems*, ed. Anthony Thwaites, London, 1988. The poem 'Church Going', p. 98. The note of 'seriousness' is the more striking in that he only comes to it out of an evident indifference. He is only 'just visiting', only goes in when sure 'there is nothing going on' and happy to be dismissive about 'up at the holy end'. Finally, however, he gives pause to his 'secular' nonchalance.

11   Why all prophethood and its culmination are so urgent belongs vitally with the Oneness of Allah as being – may we say? – 'vulnerable' to human unbelief and idolatry. Thus the *Shahadah* integrates the very unity of God with the mission of Muhammad. His being so personally named makes a mysterious nexus of his human significance with the very recognition of God as One.

12   What we may well call Quranic psalmody is collected – as doxology and invocation – in *Readings in the Qurʾan*, London, 1988, Brighton & Portland, 1999, pp. 86–112.

13   *Kufr* and *Shukr* as antonyms. For example, in 27.40 Solomon says that God is testing him 'whether he would be grateful or give the lie to God' – *a ashkur am akfar*.

14   'There is none but He' (*illa Huwa*) is the more general human formula. *La ilaha illa Anta* 'There is no god but Thou' is rare.

15   Do not 'consider' and 'consideration' derive from astronomy and the attentive study it devotes to the stars (*sidera*)? – a Creator and a creation likewise 'solicitous' of humanity, so that 'setting us over His works' is 'prizing us so highly, that we might reciprocate'. Cf. Preface and Precaution, note 18.

16   There are those who see the 'laws' we discern in these realms as actually a

sort of *islam*, an order of 'genetic' conformity by which orange-trees bear oranges, water boils or freezes, pebbles drop and fruits ripen. Only in human *islam* is the will involved.

17   Notably in the post-Hijrah situation the priority of faith-relation over blood relation entailed in the very making of the journey by Meccans to Medina. (Blood-relation could later re-assert priority once conversions to Islam had ensued.) The very vocation of often lonely prophethood demonstrated the personal bravely surmounting the tribal. Consider the Biblical doctrine of the 'remnant' – the few standing out from the throng. On Muslim 'personalism' see: Muhammad Lahbabi, *Le Personnalisme Musulman*, Paris, 1964.

18   The reality of collective wrongs will concern following chapters. It does not affect the sharply individual Quranic emphasis on sin (and judgement) and its seeming exclusion of any vicarious principle in human dealings. See below, Chapter 8.

19   The dependables of the natural order are the token of His fidelity. The moral human 'options' this sustains make 'change' a phenomenon of ours inside divine 'changlessness'. Cf. Surah 13.11: 'God does not change the things of a people until they change in themselves.' Cf. Surah 8.53.

20   The thrust of that passage about the human 'deputy' is there again in 15.26f, 38.71f, 79.27–33. Cf. also 33.72–73 about the offered 'trust' and numerous other passages celebrating the multiple provision ever serving our human purposes.

21   It is just this that the classic Muslim mind always – but needlessly – suspects, namely that there is genuine entrustment to us. Allah must be somehow thereby impaired or 'ousted' so as to be no longer *there* presiding. The error then is not to see this situation as, precisely, what He wills and wills out of the very sovereignty we fear He has relinquished. All means a more dynamic sense of what that sovereignty is. It is not a sovereignty somehow at a loss because He has a world in hand. To fear so must be a very un-Islamic fear.

22   *Dunyawi* means 'worldly': *'ilmani* is more 'lay' (as opposed to clerical); a phrase like 'related to affairs' or 'as opposed to things religious', is called for. None of these carry the precise sense implicit in our *khilafah* over 'what may be held 'religious' but only freely so, and is not, therefore, religious by duress or compulsion. It is important firmly to hold a distinction between 'a secular state' and 'secularization' as the complete rejection of religion. The former may well be compatible with a religious identity and have that identity the better for it.

23   Those unfamiliar with the term 'sacrament' may see the link readily, if they reflect on 'having the physical tell the spiritual', as for example in a kiss, a handshake, a prostration, or with flowers that 'say'.

24   'Priests and monks' are praised in, for example, e.g. 5.82, 2.62 (cf. 22.40) but they are bitterly reproached in 3.55–56, 9.31 and 57.27 ('monasticism an invention'). It is well to recall Surah 24.35–38 where the oil-fed lamp belongs with a monastic house.

25   Omitting 'the' before 'people' – as we may in this context, yet duly loyal to words recently brought back from antiquity in Christian usage.

26   In Surah 38.25 he is 'set as a vice-gerent in the earth'. He is the only

Biblical/Quranic figure so described. The long political Caliphates from Damascus to Istanbul find no mention in the Qurʾan.

27 Fazlur Rahman, *Major Themes of the Qurʾan*, Minneapolis, 1980.

28 *Ibid.*, p. 29 where he also debates how it might relate to 'conscience'. See also p. 120.

29 A view of D. H. Lawrence at least in the mouth of his Birkin in *Women in Love*, London, 1921, p. 102.

Chapter 2   Engaging Human Means to Divine Ends – The Mission of Messengers

1 *The Collected Letters of Thomas Hardy*, ed. R. L. Purdy and M. Millgate, Oxford, 1978–88, Vol. V, p. 30. Cited in: *Reading Thomas Hardy*, edited by C. P. C. Pettit, London, 1998, p. 245.

2 In many of them the command answers the frequent *yaquluna*, 'they are saying . . .', i.e. gibe or innuendo, abuse or libel Muhammad is set to counter as, in context, the urgent vindication of his integrity and that of his 'witness'. In this way we pass to 'truth through personality' – thanks to controversy about it, and 'what he is saying' is taken up into 'who is he anyway?' This becomes highly important. See below. Prophets are never merely verbalizers.

3 William Wordsworth, alike in poetry and in prose works, breathed this confidence which, if not 'theist' – in a fully Christian sense – was not 'pantheist'. In *The Prelude* he wrote of the 'great birthright of our being' as 'the spirit of religious love with which I walked with nature' (Book 2.11.271 and 257–58).

4 By appeal to the shared concept of creation, this must be true despite the distinctive slant given to its entrustness in the Hebraic terms of 'seed', land and history, via 'election' and 'covenant'. For these proceed only inside creaturely dimensions of 'humankind and the good earth' common to all toil and harvest, territory and tenure. Only the creaturely presents occasion for the word-ministry of 'messengers'.

5 Oddly so called in that how their 'pages' resulted from their words distinguishes them from those whose careers were never so recorded in verbal substance. Their attaining into 'texts' and of those 'texts' the precarious survival are obvious – if at times puzzling – tribute to their significance.

6 Monolatry, distinguished from monotheism, as worship that is singular but does not deny that other gods exist. It is likely that particular occasions – war, famine, crisis – brought 'pluralists' to appeal exclusively to 'the one' most relevant, perhaps to evoke a surer response. It seems clear that monotheism only painfully triumphed over tribal deities, with monolatry intermittently part of that story.

7 Hosea's was surely an instructive example of a wise 'strategy' of what we now think of as 'inter-faith'. He in no way connived with the falsehood in pagan credence of *baalim* presiding over earth's fertility under human hand, but he retrieved its insight (i.e. dependence, awe, gratitude) while directing it singularly to the one Yahweh, making aspects of it the raw material of its transformation.

8 In that the heart, with its fears and hopes, is not so readily dissuaded as the mind may be of illusions indulged as 'insurance policies' or wellnigh required by social pressure.

9   In that these parallels may be too roundly dismissed or discounted as if a too 'eirenic' case was being made.

10 The Word in the plural occurs only in 22.31 and 98.5 but there are some twelve allusions to them in the singular *hanif*. In single worship, 'sincerity toward Allah' and social concern, they exemplify 'true religion', as 'the *millah* of Ibrahim'.

11 *Al-Yaqin*, the Qur'an's awesome term for 'the Certain', the judgement grimly awaiting every soul and what it has 'forwarded' in life to its reckoning. There are some seven occasions of the term, cf. Surahs 15.99, 56, 95, 69.51 and 74.47. Those Biblical catastrophes could also be themes of hope and redemption in mortal times while ultimate things were more nebulous.

12 One rare example is Surah 30.3 (named after *Al-Rum*, the Eastern Rome). It notes their defeat by the Persians but promises a victory following on, within ten years.

13 See Chapter 3. Originating in Isaiah 5 and the tradition of 'a vine out of Egypt' and 'the men of Judah His pleasant plant', it occurs in all three Synoptic Gospels using the analogy of 'tenant-holders' who – by their harsh treatment of the messengers – conspire to take over the vineyard. Their behaviour has an echo in Surah 2.87 about 'messengers': 'Some they abused as liars and some they put to death.'

14 For then, there are deed and action and event as well as – or even more than – the verbal way, with history indeed affording much that is revelatory to be the substance of the verbal. Only after the Hijrah is divine action, with and around the verbal, 'revelatory' in the Qur'an. In the New Testament 'the very Word' is personified and historicized as 'truth in personality'.

15 Cf. Surahs 12.37, 20.113, 39.28, 41.3, 42.;7, 43.3, and 46.12. This sheer Arabic quality of the text and its impact was a major element, in the immediate milieu of Mecca, of its evidential warrant as truly the *risalah* of an authentic *rasul*.

16 Surahs 2.23, 10.38, or ten in 11.13 which adds: 'call upon your gods' – these being 'inventions' of theirs, rebutting the charge that his Surahs were 'inventions'. Surahs, or parts of them (as now assembled), came 'at intervals' and this also puzzled the Meccans as to what these periodic 'onsets' of utterances were.

17 The discernible analogy here is arresting – as between what Christian faith understands of the person and work of Jesus as the Christ and the Qur'an's 'nature' as at once 'eternal' and expressed in where it is thoroughly cognisable and 'possessable' in familiar human time and place to be, in Islam's case, 'word made language'.

18 Further to the previous note, this situation is close to the import of Christian credal language: 'the only begotten.' For just as the Arabic carries solely and inclusively, without remainder, the whole of divine *Wahy* as Allah's 'speech', and does so in its very particularity as no other could, so Christology understands 'the Word made flesh' as God's full initiative uniquely expressed in the person of 'His Christ'.

19 For all the eminence of Hebrew, the Bible has proved gladly translatable. Indeed its translators have brought many vernaculars into written grammars.

Christianity has neither sacred land nor sacred language, except in their capacity to be everywhere.

20   There is an intriguing parallel in the alarm the silversmiths of Ephesus felt about the possible success of Paul's mission, with its 'de-entitising' of that 'great Diana of the Ephesians': Hence the riot against him (Acts 19:23–41).

21   The technical term for 'meditation deliberately sought in solitude'. Not to be confused with *Tahannuf*, the 'way of a *hanif*'. See: *Returning to Mount Hira*, London, 1994, pp. 16–28.

22   *Innaka la ʿala khuluqin ʿazim*. Is it that he is 'of a sublime character' or that he is 'engaged in a noble task'? Either way, the re-assuring meaning is clear. See Chapter 3 on the stresses Muhammad endured.

23   'Winepress' is no exaggeration' but a valid image for all that was wrung out of him. See, e.g., John Skinner, *Prophecy and Religion: Studies in the Life of Jeremiah*, Cambridge, 1961, especially chapter xi.

Chapter 3   **The Crisis in Messenger Experience**

1   'Forlorn' seems exactly the right word here, 'quite desolate'.

2   A. B. Davidson, *Hastings Dictionary of the Bible*, Vol. ii, p. 576.

3   Surah 42.32, cf. also 55.24. Shipping became important when, in the mid Meccan time, Muhammad sent some disciples over to Ethiopia for refuge. The central theme of 'The Landscape of the Hijaz' is more fully explored in *The Event of the Qurʾan*, London, 1971, Oxford, 1994, pp. 86–97.

4   Markets sapping the will to faith are all too evident in the history of religion.

5   This entire theme could gather around Surah 73.5: 'We will cast upon thee a heavy saying.' See: *The Weight in the Word: Prophethood Biblical and Quranic*, Brighton & Portland, 1999.

6   See *Corpus Hemeticum*, ed. A. J. Festugière and A. D. Knock, Paris, 1954, IV, 23, pp. 14–16.

7   Using the term in the strict sense (small case 'i') as precisely this 'conforming' of *khilafah* to Allah's service.

8   This 'spiralling downward' can be observed in history in respect of nations and collectives of power and vested interest. When it happens with persons it is close to how Shakespeare noted 'the state of man subject to an insurrection'. *Julius Caesar*, Act 2, sc. 1, lines 67–69.

9   Thus Surah 20.115 sees Adam in the first temptation as 'weak' and 'forgetful', and lacking in staying power' (*ʿazm*). Despite the reality of the 'dominion' bestowed and of prophethood in its tuition, there is a strong tendency among Muslims to see humankind as essentially 'amenable', if not 'perfectible', in terms that would annul the very 'crisis' we are studying as implicit in that trust. That cannot be a valid account of human nature that would make superfluous the whole structure of Islam or – more incongruously still – the evidences of history at large.

10   The term was a major pre-occupation in the thought of Muhammad Kamil Husain, out of his devotion to 'peace studies' and his sense of the frail role of 'conscience' in the politics of nations. See his essay in *Mutanawwiʿat* (Miscellanies), Vol. 2, Cairo, 1958, pp. 3–28, trans. in *The Muslim World Quarterly*, Vol. 49, 3, July 1959, pp. 196–212: 'The meaning of Zulm in the

Qur'an.' The same theme is applied to the New Testament in *Qaryah Zalimah*, Cairo, 1954, Eng. trans. *City of Wrong*, Amsterdam, 1958, Oxford, 1994, using that Quranic phrase and applying it to the factors involved in the will to have Jesus crucified, seen as a supreme instance of *zulm* both religiously and politically committed. See also on Husain: *The Pen and the Faith*, London, 1985, pp. 126–44.

11 Surah 5.105 – a very significant verse addressing all 'believers', in the warning that 'reckoning awaits' but also that 'right guidance' avails so that a genuine self-responsibility obtains, as would not be the case if we were 'left on the loose' (75.36). 'You are in charge of your own souls.' How far might this liability embrace our assessment of the content of faith as distinct from our submission to its claim?

12 Notably *The Fall*, Eng. trans, 1957, tracing the hypocrisy of a self-styled 'judge-penitent' by the analogy of the fog-bound wilderness of the waterfront of Amsterdam and its circuitous canals.

13 The subverting effect of 'collectives' in overpowering the force of private conscience was a major theme of Muhammad Kamil Husain (note 10). In *Al-Wadi al-Muqaddas*, Cairo, 1968, Eng. trans., *The Hallowed Valley*, Cairo, 1977, he was very sceptical how it might be toughened to 'hold' against the corrupting influence of politics and religion.

14 *The Hallowed Valley* (note 13) drew on Surah 20.12, where, in the Qur'an's account, Moses is in *Tuwa*, the place of 'the burning bush' theophany. Cf. note 10 above and Chapter 8, note 6.

15 All is as Noah eloquently protests to God it is, in Surah 71. 'Lord day and night I have pleaded with my people, but the only effect of my pleading has been that they have fled away from it. Each time I have called them to Your forgiveness, they have put their fingers in their ears and wrapped their heads in their garments. They have persisted in arrogant stubbornness . . . How can you fail to recognize the awesome majesty of God?'

16 See Chapter 4. 'Instigated' may be too strong a term and it is only meant in the sense of 'occasioned' or 'induced'. One of the puzzling aspects of the Hijrah is that it was nowhere – it would seem – expressly commanded. It was taken by the logic after thirteen years of *balagh* – the verbal mandate which was all Muhammad thus far had – not availing to persuade more than a few in Mecca.

17 There is a sort of querulous 'Yea?' there, as if said with a leer. 'Yes, has God really said . . . ?' There is that at work which has us suspect divine 'bad faith', and prophets seem unable to disabuse us of this vicious scepticism.

18 The point is explored more in *The Event of the Qur'an*, London, 1971, Oxford, 1994, 'The Struggle to Mean', pp. 137–50.

19 The view of Fazlur Rahman, *Major Themes of the Qur'an*, Minneapolis, 1980, pp. 1–3.

Chapter 4   A Parting of the Ways – The Drama of History

1 The study has to be of these two, not of Qur'an and Bible. For the Biblical Hebrew confidence, with perceptions of 'kingship', 'nation', and – therefore

– government, rule and sovereignty – belonging to what is often called 'the Old Testament. These have their place in Chapter 5. Here we concentrate on where 'the parting of the ways' belongs and Jesus saying of that 'Old': 'It shall not be so among you' (Matthew 20:25f, Luke 22:25–27).

2   The confining of Muhammad to 'message' alone is frequent, as in 5.99, 13.40, 24.53, 29.18, 36.17 and 42.48. The *hisab*, the 'reckoning' belongs to Allah. The 'sentness' is within its contents, not beyond them.

3   The passage, among the so-called 'Songs of the Servant', is very apt to what is thought to be the 'way into being scriptured', i.e. a 'tuition' making the hearer 'one apprised of meaning', thanks to a diligent 'attention', as the condition of having a 'speaking tongue'. This 'wakening' is serial 'morning by morning' or as often the Qur'an sees it 'night by night'. Truths come as 'dawnings'.

4   This quality in the personal *Hijrah* has often been stressed by recent writers. It was also a strenuous break with the strong tradition of tribal loyalty as this is registered in pre-Islamic poetry. *Silat al-rahm*, 'the tie of the womb' or 'blood relationship' was, in a desert society, the sole assurance of security. To belong with one's clan was the very heart of duty and survival. See, e.g., A. Guillaume, *Islam*, London, 1956, p. 41.

5   There is interesting comment on the 'merit' of this Meccan powerlessness in Zakaria Bashier, *The Hijrah, Story and Significance*, Leicester, 1983. He concedes that 'in Mecca there was no ground for hypocrisy', whereas in Medina 'To be a Muslim was to ride a winning horse' (p. 71). Of the Meccan years, he writes: 'Perhaps it was that Islam needed a period of time in which to establish itself peacefully and on the merit of its own intrinsic spiritual and moral strength without the support of military force (p. 101). Why not so always?

6   Some writers detect allusions to the 'cave' tradition in 36.9 (. . . they did not see . . .') and 9.40 where the word *Shechinah* has been read in the sense of divine 'safeguarding'. Surah 59, *Al-Hashr*, however, is about another 'exile' or 'mustering' near Yathrib. Surah 18 ('the Cave') is so named for the 'Seven Sleepers of Ephesus'.

7   The last raising the issue whether 'martyrs' are 'made' in war when also taking victims, or only when 'witness unto death' is otherwise life-yielding.

8   People who sought the subversion of Islam from within by 'dissembling' a false allegiance. According to 9.107–8 there was even 'a mosque of dissent' that had to be burned down. Note also the accession of pseudo-'believers' (49.14) who had to be checked. 'Faith has not "entered your hearts".'

9   The oft-repeated phrase that captures the achievement of *Hajaru jahadu* – 'they went forth and they strove'. The clear evidences of victory were an important dimension of it. The phrase, with one or both adjectives, comes some sixteen times.

10   The 'incident' in the long Tradition is the theme of much controversy in which, either way, it is important to stress that – if there was a parley – Muhammad emerged strictly loyal. Some commentary will not allow that he could ever have been thus tempted: other that, being so, he was all the more vindicated. The words 'they are but names . . .' 'inventions' (53.43) *could* fit either way, as a concessionary formula *or* as a rejectioning assertion. The

passage underlies Salman Rushdie's notorious and malicious *The Satanic Verses*, London, 1988.

11 Though the apparent 'negotiability' of Muhammad keenly dismayed his most ardent followers who may not have recognised what his strategy was. For the moment access to Mecca turned on Quraishi compliance – a situation soon to end. 'Umar, for example, protested: 'Is he not Allah's Apostle and are we not Muslims and are they not polytheists? . . . Why should we agree to what is demeaning to our religion?' Ibn Ishaq: *Sirat Rasul Allah*, trans. A. Guillaume, Oxford, 1957, p. 504.

12 The title of Khalid Muhammad Khalid's study, Cairo, 1958 – *Ma'an 'ala-l-Tariq Muhammad wa-l-Masih*.

13 Using a ready and popular adaptation of Matthew 6:33 about 'seeking first the Kingdom . . .' with the belief that only by power would 'the other things' be 'added'. This was the third 'temptation' offered to Jesus in the desert – and rejected.

14 It is not possible to translate *biazetai* as if the kingdom was forcing its way. The verb's form can only mean 'was being forcibly treated' (passive). It is not that 'the kingdom has been coming violently.' Cf. *harpazo* in John 6:14–15 and the always sinister sense in Luke 16:16. 'The Kingdom' was already so present as to have political activists try to adopt it to their own ends. 'Violence' does not describe God at work (cf. Matthew 11:29). For a contrary view, see: G. E. Ladd: *Jesus and the Kingdom*, London, 1964, pp. 155f.

15 Ibn Khaldun: *Al-Muqaddimah*, trans. F. Rosenthal, Vol. 1, Princeton, 1958, pp. 187f and 322 and 414.

16 The same is differently true in the faith-content and the community-shape of Islam. In its narrative of events, the Qur'an is also rehearsing what transpired in the identity-making of the faithful. The Hijrah, purposes in Yathrib, Badr, Uhud and beyond are alike waymarks in the movement to completion of the Qur'an *and* of participatory Muslims in their allegiance. Each *fitnah*, for example, that occurs for them belongs in its themes.

17 Further, the whole crux of his conversion lies in the fact that – as he recollected – the voice from heaven did not say: 'I am Christ' – as any devout Jew might expect such a 'heavenly voice' to say, speaking from those 'heights' where precisely 'a Christ' could be expected to be 'riding on clouds of power'. The point was that 'the voice' from that 'Messianic' place actually identified itself with 'this Jesus' whom Saul 'persecuted'. The whole logic of what happened to him is in that clue.

18 Except insofar as the *wahy* from which it had mediation did fuse with the exchanges earlier studied, of charge and rebuttal, between the Quraish and Muhammad.

19 So much in the impulse to 'epistle-writing' and sending is of this order, aiming to integrate the dispersed into a common discipline and to steer them through many cultural dangers.

20 *Al-Muqaddimah* (note 15), Vol. 1, pp. 473f.

21 G. Bornkamm: *Early Christian Experience*, London, 1969, p. 21.

Chapter 5   Sympathy Engaging with Antipathy – Power and Faith

1   Trying to relate the Bible and the Qur'an is only a feasible purpose for Christians if we have the former finally assessed in New Testament terms. This admittedly leaves aside the issue of the Bible's 'unity'. Otherwise there would be outstanding areas of the Hebrew Bible quite altering the perspective here.

2   It is often stressed in the Arab world that the two faiths have co-existed amicably enough through long years. At one level that may be true enough and deserves recognition but – with exceptions and for the most part – it was not a co-existence that squarely broached what most divided them.

3   The familiar phrase in so many apostolic Letters and, by its frequent usage and inclusive shape, the embryo of later Creeds.

4   'They did not esteem Allah the truth of His esteeming' is the case the Qur'an brings three times against the polytheists (Surahs 6.91, 22.74 and 39.67); the verb *qadara* 'to weigh' or to 'measure', 'to have a worthy comprehension of', is equally at risk and at stake in the custody of Scriptures.

5   It is strange that of late this passage – so plainly a mutual repudiation of incompatible worships – is cited as if it were a statement about mutually acceptable ones that could readily co-exist in a sort of 'ecumenical' respect, merely agreeing to differ. See, for example, *The Qur'an; An Introduction*, Mohammad Abu-Hamdiyyah, London, 2000, pp. 53, 107. There are other verses from which to argue that hope and attitude, like 5.48, 2.148, and 49, 13.

6   Pakistan is the most single twentieth-century evidence of the will of Muslims to seek and enjoy political power, being a state founded expressly in the name of being 'Islamic'. As its first half-century so painfully revealed, it has struggled both to define and to realise what 'the Islamic State' should be.

7   In *De civitate Dei*, V. 15, he saw the Roman Empire as having been entrusted by God, before the advent of Christ, with preparing universal Empire from whose 'virtues of the hard road' the Church itself had found its ultimate occasion.

8   Surah 48.29 affirms that 'the religion of truth' is meant to 'be victorious over all religion'.

9   This is not to argue blandly that 'faith is only sound when under duress'. See below, but as Muslim writers have observed, Islam in Mecca made more demands of a deeply religious order on adherents than did post-Hijrah circumstance, where the demands were more of a physical order and 'being Muslim' had more and more the sanction of success.

10   This 'pledging' that all human life is 'in God and to God' is a universal 'acknowledging', not as at Sinai a particular 'covenant' about a land endowed on a people. The question is in the negative: 'Am I not . . . ?' Implying (as all such questions do) an affirmative answer, but awaiting it. See *Am I not your Lord? Human Meaning in Divine Question*, London, 2002.

11   Surah 30.30 – a pivotal verse which bids Muhammad 'Give your whole being devotedly to the things of faith as a man of pure religion, the faith God made proper to mankind by His creation of them.' *Fitrah* has almost the single sense of 'nature' (in humans) and the 'nature' of religion whereby each is suited to

the other, so that to be *muslim* is to be duly human and duly human to be *muslim*. This seems to underwrite the case here that faith comes within our *khilafah* – though the argument about what is 'natural' is ever open.

12 Hence the urgent language of 30.30: 'Set your face towards . . .' or, religion and selfhood as things of 'divine seriousness', with an honest realism about the reach of evil.

13 The *la* in the *Shahadah* is that of 'absolute negation', so that 'there is not' has to mean 'there can never be . . .' other than Allah. Do not all faiths claim, or allege, the same about what they hold 'ultimate'?

14 Echoing the wariness T. S. Eliot ascribes to the mind of Becket when he visualizes the power his very martyrdom will wield over his foes. He cannot even suffer without sin. Self-seeking may beset the martyr no less than any other self. No 'holiness' is immune. T. S. Eliot, *Murder in the Cathedral*, London, 1968 edn., p. 48.

15 Matthew 22:21, Mark 12:17, Luke 20:25, in Jesus' response to the lawyer's query about 'tribute in taxation'. It was a loaded question, given the hated Roman occupation. Jesus was being invited to walk into the trap of saying: 'Do – or – do not pay them', in either case 'separating the politics that paid' (approving Caesar) or that which would not pay (disowning him) from any business with Jewish religion.

16 Is it not precisely because nature yields the sciences' 'neutral' potential that we can be 'spiritual' at all? Microphones do not discriminate between users, thwarting liars and only functioning for honest folk.

17 The phrase *Ummatan wasatan* in Surah 2.143 has been endlessly studied. Does it mean Arabs occupying 'middle earth' or – in the context about the change of *Qiblah* now set at Medina, between Mecca and Jerusalem or, again, Muslims as a people with balanced ethics? as noted in Preface and Precaution, note 4.

18 From Alexander to Napoleon, 'this is the way of them'. All Muslim régimes have been inherently expansionist from the Umayyads, the Ottomans, to the Mughals in their sub-continent, likewise successive 'Christendoms' fulfilled in the 'making of subject peoples'.

19 Is it only a fond idealism that sees 'peacemakers as the children of God'? Or is it only realism to know that breeders of enmity, brooders on combat, instigators of battle, are not 'kindred of God'?

20 That any 'favour' done to Muhammad – as crude allegiance might argue – was 'favour' done to God was religiously a *non sequitur* as the Surah was at pains to insist. But why should there have been the reason to think so in the first place – the reason lying in the clear junction in the armed succour for which *both* were heard to plead?

21 Not invariably so. For with the cumulative experience of denial of power, the Shi'ah developed their concept of *taqiyyah* or 'quietism', but as a necessary position of 'non-resistence' for the time being, without foregoing the right to rebel at some later, more propitious time.

22 Richard Hooker (1554–1600) was the great apologist of the Elizabethan Anglican 'solution' to State/Church issues – grand, reasonable, spacious and eirenic. His *The Laws of Ecclesiastical Polity*, Oxford, 1841 edn, was his great legacy. See discussion – also of Coleridge, Burke and Gladstone – in:

The Education of Christian Faith, Brighton & Portland, 2000, Chapter 5, pp. 82–101.

23 Surah 7.172 imagines all humankind as a simultaneous audience, antecedent even to the Noahid 'covenant' and still more to that of Sinai.

24 Trans. Nigel Griffin, London, 1992. Born in 1474, Las Casas died in 1566. While he did not question Spain's political rights, sanctioned by the Papacy, he passionately preached the moral duty they involved. He found philosophical support from the University of Salamanca. See also Anthony Pagden, *Peoples and Empires*, London, 2001, pp. 69–87.

25 See, for example, Susan Billington Harper *In the Shadow of the Mahatma*, Grand Rapids, 2000.

26 Benjamin Disraeli, *Tancred*, London, 1844, VI, iii, where and also in *Lothair* he indulged his Semitic theory of 'a destined race.'

27 For régimes that ground themselves in the legitimacy of *their* shape of the faith they espouse will always be prey to partisans of differing versions. Theology and politics are still more embroiled.

Chapter 6   Holy Writ and the Writ of Readers

1 Though Muslims would insist that *hifz* in the sense of 'having by heart' is at the core of their duty to the text. There is also a rigorous – if highly artistic – 'keeping' to the letter in the craft of calligraphy. Veneration is always much more than academic, if academic at all. There is also the question whether texts are for 'keeping' in view of meanings still to be awaited (cf. Isaiah 8:16). See below.

2 *Ahl al-Kitab* in the Qur'an denotes 'Israel and Israelites' and, sometimes Christians (Surahs 2.105, 2.109, 3.64f, 4.123, 5.15, 5.68, 29.46, 33.26, 57.29, 59.2, 98.1 and 6 – all but Surah 29 being listed as Medinan, when hostility supervened on expectation.

3 Surahs 4.82 and 47.24. Cf 23.68 and 38.29 where the Qur'an, sent as *mubarak* ('benediction'), awaits 'men of understanding'.

4 It is noteworthy that when the artist Vincent Van Gogh first ventured to be a Christian preacher, at a Chapel in England, this was his text. There was deep pathos in his choice.

5 See, for example, John Holden: *The Collection of the Qur'an*, Cambridge, 1977 and the writings of John Wansbrough, e.g. *Quranic Studies, Sources & Methods of Scriptural Interpretation*, Oxford, 1977, and the long debate ensuing from Joseph Schacht's *Introduction to Islamic Law*, Oxford, 1964. See also recent reviewing in Harold Motzki, ed., *The Biography of Muhammad: The Issue of Sources*, Leiden, 2000.

6 The ultimate principle of arrangement in Surahs of diminishing length remains puzzling, in that it defies chronology, seeing that – by style criteria – the short, poetic, ecstatic pieces were the earliest yet come latest. The thirty/sixty divisions for recitative reading are quantitative. There is also the likelihood that some longer Surahs are composite and 'astride' the Hijrah.

7 Explanations have been many and, some, ingenious – the initials of fragment-owners, initial letters of prominent words, symbols of 'verbalism' or of

'matchless Arabic', etc. See Morris Seale, *Qur'an and Bible*, London, 1978, 'The Mysterious Letters of the Qur'an', pp. 29–46.

8 On the Qur'an as an 'event', see my study: *The Event of the Qur'an*, London, 1971, Oxford, 1994, the 'event' quality being unique to Muhammad in entire contrast to the communal matrix of the New Testament discussed elsewhere.

9 It seems clear that the purpose of the 'Canon', in part, was to exclude material which was eventuating, like gnostic versions of Christhood, that might jeopardise the Church's faith. The anxieties were akin to those underlying the sense for the necessity of creeds.

10 Except perhaps for *Hadith Qudsi* which, according to some scholars enjoy a status higher than Tradition at large. It has sometimes been observed that the Gospels are – as it were – the *Ahadith* (pl.) of Christianity, as sayings and events of a central figure. It is, however, only a loose comparison and reflects how that central (Christian) figure, being 'truth through personality', is necessarily within Scripture, whereas *Hadith* in Islam must differ from the verbatim text in which and as which the Qur'an 'houses' revelation.

11 The issue might be studied in the debate between B. S. Childs, *Introduction to the Old Testament as Scripture*, Yale, 1979 and James Barr, *Holy Scripture, Canon, Authority and Criticism*, London, 1983.

12 Having to do with the Nativity narratives in Surahs 3 and 19, controversies around the crucifixion, the possible allusion to the Eucharist and the disciples as Jesus' *ansar*, and the Jesus/'Isa dual name.

13 See note 3 above. *Tadabbur* comes as close as any term could to the 'read, mark, learn and inwardly digest' of Christian liturgy.

14 The root is very frequent. 'Esteem' is probably the surest in the theological context, the 'divine Names' being less than worthily comprehended, weighed, acknowledged. See Surahs 6.91, 22.74 and 39.67. Cf. Chapter 5, note 4.

15 Cf. Shabbir Akhtar: *Be Careful with Muhammad*, London, 1989, Chap. 5, where he castigates those who admit elements of 'fallibility,' in any sphere, in the Scripture which is their 'ultimate referent' for faith . . .' to coincide exactly with the wishes of contemporary Christian theology' (p. 97), adding: 'If a book can be fallible in its claims about astronomy and biology, there is no reason why it should be infallible in its pronouncements on religious doctrine.'

16 Defined in the *OED* as 'versed in Scripture' or 'relying on it alone for religious belief'. 'Scriptuary' would be a preferred word here meaning simply 'possessed of holy writ'.

17 Paul's term in Philippians 2.7–8 – a 'self-emptying' not as relinquishing what is then no longer there, but foregoing (e.g. 'majesty') for a congruent purpose so that, while not abandoned it is still there in seeming forfeiture (cf. 'This is our God, the Servant-King'). Something of such a generous 'self-foregoing' is present in the Biblical/Quranic version of a 'creaturehood' appointed to 'delegacy' for God in custody of His created order.

18 Fazlur Rahman, *Major Themes of the Qur'an*, Minneapolis, 1980, p. 3.

19 Lit., 'Make Him great a greatly making.' The verse uses the intensive form, or 'absolute accusative', where the root verb supplies its own root noun. The effect is to 'mean' intensely. Cf. 'being exceeding sorrowful', i.e., 'sorrowing a sorrow'.

20 *Ibid.*, p. 29. The relation of 'conscience', whether personal or collective, to 'holy writ' with 'revelation', has always been problematic for a theological ethics. On the one hand, how can human conscience presume to 'improve upon', still less to 'override', divine will revealed? Yet, given all the areas – many and increasing – on which such 'holy writ' is, or seems, silent, may we not have to see conscience as within 'caliphate', so that it might somehow share with 'holy writ'? Has it not been happening so all the time?

21 Arthur Jeffery, *The Foreign Vocabulary of the Qur'an*, Baroda, 1938. Legitimate enough as an academic aspect of the Qur'an's being 'pure Arabic' and Arabic alone, it examined terms traceable to non-Arabic roots, such as Hebrew, Aramaic, Ethiopic. It caused something of a stir at the time (published in India) as calling in question a dogma of the Qur'an about itself. What was more needed was the Arabic vocabulary as the positive medium – and vindication – of a revelatory role, i.e. the real import of the Arabicity as here in mind.

Chapter 7   The Time and Place Factor

1 The *Sirah* being the life of Muhammad, dating indeed from his birth, but essentially comprising the years between *c.* 609 and 632, the onset of 'Qur'an recipience' and his death. This *mise-en scène* is so clearly in contrast to that of the ages-long spread of Biblical contents. Strictly inside the *wahy* experience of his *Sirah*, however, are long vistas of previous 'messengers' and their receptions, as well as echoes of Biblical biographies and of elements from the Apocrypha – 'Gog and Magog', etc. and *Dhu-al-Qarnain*. These give their ancient aura to the Qur'an as Muhammad's.

2 'About something more ultimate than itself' applies to the New Testament. The Hebrew Bible, however, for all its 'historicisation' of truth, does contain elements of verbatim utterance, saying 'God's speech'.

3 See, e.g., Jalal al-Din al-Suyuti: *Al-Itqan fi 'Ulum al-Qur'an*, Cairo, 3rd printing, 1941, 1st Part, section 9, pp. 39–43. Surah 8 relates clearly to the encounter at Badr (with allusions in Surah 3) while sundry occasions late in Medina are clue to verses in Surah 9.

4 John Dryden: *The Poems of*, ed. John Sargeant, Oxford, 1935, 'Absalom and Achitophel, Part 1, p. 56, Dryden's satirical sarcasm at the expense of the Biblical Zimri (1 Kings 16) who – in a borrowing of the story of rebellion against David – is made to figure the Duke of Buckingham in the reign of Charles II. Taken out of Dryden's innuendo, it strikes a chord about religions supposedly comprising all that 'reality' requires they be.

5 The Christian 'case' here would be that 'this Christ of God' in the entire context of creation, human 'caliphate' and the *zulm* of human history 'comprises' the utmost measure of what God is *vis-à-vis* the real measure of human reality as present in 'the sin of the world' as the Cross enshrines it. God 'finds us in being thus found in His Christ'. A veritable summation.

6 A fair conjecture though the dating of the Book of Ruth is unclear. A story of 'the days of the Judges' – whose dismal features it much relieves – it takes pains to explain archaic details and certainly counters how urgent to Nehemiah was the preserving of racial purity.

7 Perhaps too often missed but the more arresting. Hosea 1:9: 'You are not My
   people and I am not the "I AM" you think I am,' plays on the word of Exodus
   3:14, the sheet-anchor of the confidence that Yahweh had been, and would
   for ever remain, whom as 'theirs' that Exodus had shown Him to be. The
   Hebrew often rendered as a philosophic riddle: 'I am that I am': is more truly
   read as: 'I will be there as who there I will be.' The event, lived through, is
   the only clue to answer the people's question as to guarantee. Hosea calls this
   'He and us' into radical question.

8 I.e., 'the abrogator' and 'the abrogated'. The doctrine hinges on, e.g., Surah
   13.38–39.

   'To no messenger was it given to bring any sign unless by leave of God.
   For every era there is a book. God annuls and confirms what He wills
   and with Him is *Umm al-Kitab*.' (Meccan)
      Surah 16.101 adds:
   'When We exchange one verse in place of another – and God knows
   what He sends in revelation – they say: 'You are just making it up your-
   self.' (Meccan) These seem to indicate that his audience was perplexed
   by what they thought inconsistent. Surah 2.106 (Medinan) says that
   when Allah abrogates or causes a verse to be forgotten, He brings
   instead one 'better' or akin, being 'able to do all things'. It is fair to
   ask how that 'cause to be forgotten' *nunsiha na'ti bi-khairin minha*
   comes about.

   Jalal al-Din al-Suyuti in his *Al-Itqan* expounds *naskh* in Vol. 2, section 47,
   pp. 33–44, Cairo, 1941.

9 In that the 'reckoning' (*hisab*) around *balagh* is with Allah alone, whereas –
   post-Hijrah – it is, at least partially, taken up by Islam's own campaign as
   duly 'reckoning' with the Meccan obduracy in martial terms. The instinct of
   the Medinan Qur'an is that such was the case. Whereas 13.40 – in Mecca –
   had told Muhammad that he might die before he saw *hisab* (clearly not death
   in campaigning) and re-iterating, 'Your sole task is *al-balagh*'.

10 In that pagan 'diversion' of love and worship from Allah alone on to rocks,
   or wells, or high peaks, or tribal rituals, or multiple daimonisms, becomes the
   modern absolute that 'worships' gain, race, money, commodity ('that bias of
   the world') or the ever avid self, collective or private. To deny and denounce
   these, God might well 'cause us to forget' (2.106) need for the cruder
   disavowal of the primitive sort.
      Are there not also moral violations which power, by its lights or means,
   can neither identify nor end?

11 Surahs 56.60 and 70.41. In context they seem to mean that Allah is not to be
   'eluded' by those who think to escape death and retribution. But divine
   'never-outdatedness' is surely a Quranic truth undergirding the finality of
   'revelation'.

12 See Muhammad Kamil Husain, *Mutanawwi'at*, Cairo, 1958, Vol. 2, pp.
   29–34. He describes this pseudo-scientific approach to the Qur'an as 'A
   stupid heresy' (*Bid'ah Hamqa'*).

13 See his, *The Reconstruction of Religious Thought in Islam*, Lahore, 1934.
   The literature of his thought and poetry is voluminous. Cf. Iqbal Singh: *The
   Ardent Pilgrim, An Introduction to His Life and Work*, London, 1951.

14 Muhammad Asad in his *The Message of the Qur'an*, Gibraltar, 1980, combines the two, translating *Al-Rabb* as 'the Sustainer', God being 'the fosterer and sustainer of all creation' – objective as well as conceptual – and therefore the ultimate source of all authority, p. 2.

15 If the politicised term, as English applies it by transliteration, only to the office of Muhammad's ruling successors, can be employed to denote – in us all – the privilege examined here throughout.

16 See his *Novum Organum*, sections xlix to lxvi, '. . . the mischievous authorities of systems, which are founded either on common notions, or on a few experiments, or on superstition'. He lists 'Idols of the Tribe' (deceptions of the senses), 'Idols of the Cave' (partiality or favouring of preferences), 'Idols of the Market-place' (false use of words), and 'Idols of the Theatre' (popular distortions). Bacon (1561–1626) was using *eidoloi* in an idiosyncratic way, concerning philosophical self-deception. There is irony in that his sort of *eidoloi*, when erected by deluded selfhoods in realms political and economic and collective, are nefarious and damnable, not merely delusory. 'Cave and Tribe and Market-place and Theatre' are then more sinister and deadly. See below.

17 See a careful study of the 'land dimension' in Judaism in: W. D. Davies: *The Territorial Dimension of Judaism*, 2nd edn., Minneapolis, 1991.

18 Notably the prophet's advice to exiles in Chapter 29. See also a classic study in John Skinner, *Prophecy and Religion, Studies in the Life of Jeremiah*, Cambridge, 1961.

19 Would it be unfair to infer that from the troubles the third century Church had, in its sundry councils, around the lapsed under persecution and the vexed questions that resulted about 're-baptism' and/or 'the one baptism' of the later Nicene Creed? When Cyprian, Bishop of Carthage (d. 258) wrote in *Sentt. Epp*, 'None of us makes himself a Bishop of bishops or obliges his colleagues . . . to any necessity of obedience . . .' he threw light on a situation imperial order would aim to undertake.

20 That 'other will' being the policy of the Palestine Liberation Organisation to hold its mind 'secular' (see its 'National Charter) in not being identified solely with Islam or with Islam in sharply 'Medinan' terms.

21 One recent, random example would be Mark Allen Powell, *Chasing the Eastern Star: Adventures in Biblical Response Criticism*, Louisville, 2001. Or the Hebrew writer, Amos Oz, writes provocatively in: *The Story Begins: Essays on Literature*, trans. M. Bar-Tura, London, 1999:

> 'The game of reading requires you, the reader, to take an active part, to bring to the field your own life experience and your own innocence, as well as caution and cunning . . .' (p. 115)

Muslims would not agree nor Christians, in that Scripture is not a 'game'. Yet many non-Muslims have brought their 'innocence' to the Qur'an, unaware of what was required of them in its appreciation. As Oz adds (p.16), 'Without a patient ear one cannot hear . . . unless one internalises the details.'

22 That sentiment will be more familiar in 'Reformed' circles in the Christian tradition. It is, however, not uncongenial to the Qur'an's repeated plea for *qawmun yatafakkarun*, 'A people with their wits about them.'

23 For New Testament people, for example, the injunction among several like

ones in Romans 12:18: 'If it is possible, as much as lies in you, be at peace with all.' Perhaps the most inclusive of several Quranic *ayat* about inter-communal mutuality would be 2.148: *Fa-stabiqu al-khairat*, 'Seek to excel one another in good works.' This follows the words: 'Every rite has a prayer direction to which it turns.' This *may* underwrite even diversity of religious liturgy. In any event, there are many allusions to a divine intention in, and assent to, religio-communal diversity (5.48, 11.118, 16.93, 42.8, cf. also 5.43).

24 The drastic flux of twentieth-century oil wealth into segments of the Islamic world tests that faith's capacity to nourish these countering qualities no less than faiths elsewhere. 'You are liable for your own selves' – as we have seen – is the mandate of Surah 5.105. The concept of *zulm al-nafs*, 'self-wronging', would certainly comprise the antitheses of 'the lowly in heart' caring for *itmi'nan* at 'the remembrance of God.'

25 Shakespeare's familiar phrase in *King John*, Act 2, Sc. 1, line 575, using 'commodity', not as *res materia* merely, but the lust to possess and oppress, to turn all to self-advantage regardless of what integrity owes to all.

There have been remarkable strides in the adaptation of Islamic banking to contemporary situations by subduing the merely acquisitive to the truly participatory. There are widespread efforts to agree on *Shari'ah*-compliant measures and by them to penetrate financial servicing, even insurance, right across the Islamic world and its western diaspora. The Zam Zam time share tower in Mecca itself is a notable example of venturesome initiatives. See *Pioneer News*, Impact Media (Europe) Ltd, London, 2003.

26 Among the most powerful exposition of this theme – of humanity in the 'will to power' as 'the only creature who refuses to be what he (man) is' – is Albert Camus, *The Rebel*, trans. Anthony Bower, rev. edn. New York, 1956. He ponders whether the will to power is not inherently self-destructive, or whether – never being innocent – it can find and obey a 'principle of reasonable culpability' (p. 11). The latter is less likely if its auspices are religious. For these invoke an 'absolute'.

27 A supreme example of a religious faith being the more ethically political by being itself non-political must be the great Hebrew prophets – an Amos, a Hosea, an Isaiah, a Jeremiah, each the more incisive because they were the less allied.

28 Surah 2.30f, translating that *'alam ma la ta'lamun*, 'I know what you know not.'

Chapter 8   In the End – God

1 The sense of harsh dismay which the Qur'an's 'Last things' kindles for non-Muslim readers – to be explored below – stems from the absence in the divine 'mercy' (present over all) of any dimension of vicarious suffering, the dimension which has central place in the Biblical meaning of 'Messiah' and in the resulting New Testament emphasis on 'redemption'. The point, more deeply, has to await a logic of reflection.

2 In that there is 'guilt' for each and all in the wrongs committed by collectives

and there can be an assumed 'innocence' of the individual in that his/her 'share' in these wrongs was so infinitesimal, or ambivalent, or inevitable as to be discounted. Yet it belongs to us in any honest light.

3 The Buddhist scheme indeed posits responsible 'selfhood' in the obligations of compassion and of 'The Eightfold Path', but on the basis of an essential 'passing away' into 'oceanic non-being'. This makes any notion of, or desire for, personal immortality the oddest illusion of all. Or would the Hindu say that all the Semites have meant by 'last judgement' proceeds via the incidence of *karma*, graduating futures higher or lower according to implicit worth?

4 The negative is not quite absolute, but almost so. Surah 6.51 says 'there is no protecting friend, no intercessor, other than He'. 'Other than He there is neither friend nor intercessor' (6.69, cf. 35.43). Surah 74.48 says: 'The mediation of no mediator avails them then', i.e. in *al-Saʾir*. Does 21.28 imply that *shafaʿah* might avail for those whom Allah accepts?, when it would be unnecessary. Popular piety, however, has credited the intercession of the Prophet, patriarchs, saints and 'holy ones'. See below and the related absence of vicarious suffering 'bearing' evils done and the concept of singular liability before God.

5 *Wazara* means to carry, or undertake, a burden, and yields *wazir*, an 'officer', or 'minister', *kallafa* (second form) 'to entrust' or 'assign a task' to.

6 The theme of *zulm* in the Qurʾan often occupied the thought and work of Muhammad Kamil Husain. In *Qaryah Zalimah* ('City of Wrong'), Cairo, 1954, Eng. trans., Amsterdam, 1958, he studied how personal conscience was so often over-ridden by collective vested interest, advocating a resolute private determination not to let this happen by holding private conscience firm against all odds. The guilt of collectives must surely be also in the reckoning of 'the Last Day', no less than individual sins.

7 Cf. Surah 80.33f. 'When the blast is heard on a Day when a man will flee from his brother, from his mother and his father, from his wife and sons – on that Day every man will be solely absorbed in what is at stake about him.'

8 Hosea's vivid imagery (2:15) of hope against the ghastly toll of retributive violence told in Joshua 7 around the 'sin' of Achan, flouting Joshua's gruesome edict of mass slaughter.

9 See below. The central figure, *Al-Dajjal*, or 'Anti-Christ', does not have mention in the Qurʾan but 21.96 speaks of the 'loosing of yaʾjuj and maʾjuj', Gog and Magog, the subversive powers of evil. The slaying of *Al-Dajjal* by Jesus, who becomes a Muslim on his 'return', was drawn from a Muslim versioning of Christian eschatology during centuries of inter-action. See: Norman Daniel: *Islam and the West: The Making of an Image*, rev. edn. Oxford, 1993, Appendix C, pp. 347–8, 'Christ and the Last Day'.

10 The Meccan Surahs have many allusions to this insistent pagan incredulity about the resuscitation of their bones, their limbs and identities. Life and its meaning were so totally enshrined in the precarious daily 'breathing' of life. The old Hebraic sense of 'once to live' was of a more wistful order. Cf. Psalm 39:13: 'O spare me a little . . . before I go hence and be no more.' Always for the Jew, though not for the Quraish, was the sense of 'covenant' and 'election' and, thence, a divine concern with human brevity. These could ripen towards those other psalmists, singing: 'I shall be satisfied when I awake after

Thy likeness' (17:15) – assuming we know how to date the Psalter.

11   Though his 'heart sinks' at what his 'friends' say, Job's sense of divine justice persuades him that, somehow, he will set satisfied eyes on his 'vindicator', whether still 'in flesh' in mortal terms or, somehow, in 'other flesh', the physical being so crucial to the real. The ethical must control the mystery.

12   It is out of the inner tension between 'things covenanted' and situations morally violated by the harsh enigmas of circumstance that the psalmist is brought to this sublime conviction.

13   It seems pointless to ask How soon? or how long? when death has supervened.

14   If Surah 96 be the inaugural one, it is there already (96.2), our common genesis via a sperm-clot. Repeatedly there is this emphasis on the mystery – and trust – of human wombing and the sexual exercise of *khilafah* as vital to all else. Hence also the Qur'an's horror at infanticide (Surah 81.8–9; cf. 16.59).

15   The root *batala*, to be 'in vain, futile, null, empty, false', with its derivatives, is very frequent. The divine ends in creation and the entrustment of humankind cannot go unvindicated or stay in question. Cf. Surah 8.7–8: 'God meant to verify the truth of his words by the total rout of the truth rejectors, demonstrating how true the truth is and how vain the falsehood, however much the sinners may detest it.' The immediate context is the evident vindication of Islam, and Muhammad's strategy, at the battle of Badr. The issue for all scriptural eschatology is – 'how true the truth is' – emerges in 'the Last Day'.

16   That is, the whole significance of Jesus in ministry, death and risen-ness as 'realising' the Messianic meaning and doing so definitively beyond all the ambiguities and dubieties in the long nurture of that hope. In the very nature of things, that 'secret' could only be known and told in the witness and the formulation of the Church's mind of which it was both clue and cause. That it was always latent or implicit in the story is evident in the fabric of the Gospels written in its sequel.

17   This mortal awareness of that post-mortal *eschaton*, ethics as eschatology, is well analysed in Fazlur Rahman: *Major Themes of the Qur'an*, Minneapolis, 1980, pp. 106–20. See note 26 below.

18   The roots, 'to return' and 'to become' are frequent. Life is a theme of moral becoming, towards a 'destination' of final register sealing the process. 'To Him are we returning' or (passive) 'Being brought again', imply no absence of God. They speak His ever-presence in its ethical, judgemental quality as moving into 'destiny'.

19   This through all the variants, Pauline, Petrine, Johannine and 'Hebrews' as a letter-treatise, is the New Testament consensus.

20   It could be said that this exchange between Jesus and 'terrorist X?' was, indeed, the first (hence 'original') recognition of the heart of a suffering Christology and so of theology also and of a consonant eternal 'this day with me in paradise'.

21   The Greek, and Aramaic, sense does *not* admit what the mystics love – 'the God within'. The meaning is that the Kingdom is actively at work 'within your ranks', 'in your affairs', in the here and now of your politics and culture.

22 Revelation 22:4. 'Hard-labouring' in all the turbulence of his mind and imagery – and of his millennial exegetes.

23 Paul in 1 Corinthians 15:24–26 sees Christ in this central role moving ever within the ultimate sovereignty of God alone.

24 Some of them came via St Ephraem. See Arent Jan Wensinck: *Handbook of Early Muhammadan Tradition*, Leiden, 1927. All stem from a sense of some 'dynamism' in evil and how it might ever be terminated either in time, or beyond time. One might cite Søren Kierkegaard in his different context of *The Sickness unto Death* (1849), Eng. trans. 1989: 'Works arising in sin gain strength and power only through sin . . . Deep within itself sin has a consistency . . .' Paragraphs XI.129–XI.207. See: H. V. Hong and E. H. Hong, eds: *The Essential Kierkegaard*, Princeton, 1995, pp. 361–71. *Al-Dajjal*, or 'arch deceiver', often 'the Anti-Christ', symbolises this 'scheming' wrongness.' He/it may be 'loosed' terribly, to be then subdued a thousand years, only to return and be at last consigned evermore to hell. In that scenario Muslim tradition has a role for 'Jesus', returning as a Muslim, to die and come to a grave in Medina. *Al-Dajjal* and the Jesus of this eschatology are unknown to the Qur'an.

25 *She'ol*, in that Biblical concept, being so nebulous and shadowy a condition, some confidence in bodily 'resurrection' came to seem essential to any emphasis on continuing moral liability after death – without which the idea of 'judgement' and/or reward or requital could have no meaning. Yet the nature of that new 'bodiliness', as necessary to any ongoing personal identity, has always been – and will doubtless ever remain – problematic, eluding explanation.

26 For New Testament faith this issue is bound up with reading 'the empty tomb' of Jesus and the meaning of his Resurrection. For Muslims it has meant reflection on the 'physicality' of 'the Fire' and 'the Garden' in the Qur'an. Are they 'allegorical' in the sense meant by the distinction in Surah 3.7? If 'actual/literal' – as is mostly believed – we keep the sharp ethical problems already noted. These become the more vexing in that 'the ethical' was precisely the point in the eschatological. Fazlur-Rahman in *Major Themes* (note 17), pp. 112–13, seems equivocal: 'There are thus literal *psycho-physical effects* of the Fire, without there being a literal fire.'

Index of Names and Terms

Index of Names and Terms

Index of Names and Terms

Index of Names and Terms

Index of Names and Terms

Index of Themes

Note: Terms and themes recurrent in the central focus of the case here for a 'scriptural unison' around God and humankind within the natural (and sacramental) order are not included among THEMES – e.g. creation, creaturehood, prophethood, caliphate (human), and religion.

Index of Themes

Index of Themes

Index of Themes

signs, x, 3, 7, 10, 28, 29, 68, *see also ayat*
sin, dynamic in, 33, 34, 57, 58, 97, 130
sincerity, 61, *see also ikhlas*
slavery, in the New Testament, 50
Son, the – significance in, 33, 34
sovereignty, divine, 1, 2, 9, 62, 75, 76
   and human power, 56, 88, 109, 114
'spoils of war', 61
State, the, 35, 44, 58, 60
   and Hebrew prophets, 28
   in Islam, 53, 121
   the secular, 64
submission, 2, 26, 55, 57, 59, *see also*
   islam
   how feasible?, 25
subversion, political, 84
suffering, 45, 47, 63
   of messengers, 27, 28, 44
suspicion, of God, 36, 37
   inter-human, 60, 73, 83, 87, 114,
   118, *see also zann*

task, the reading, 65f, 82
technology, ix, 85, 86, 93
techniques, xii, 85, 86
theocracy, illusion of, 87
'things of Caesar,' the, 58, 59, 121
'things of God,' the, 58, 59, 121
time and place, 79f
   patriarchal, 70
   prophetic, 70
tolerance, 56, 83
Tradition, 40, 43, 71
   Islamic, 99, 100, 123, 130, *see also*
   Hadith
tragedy, 75
transcendence, 5, 9, 78, 81, 83
translation, 28, 68
   issues in, 22, 116
'travail of the soul', 28, 30, 47
truth, love of, 57
   politicization of, 62
   and time, 80f

unity, divine, 2, 18, 23
universe, too vast?, 15
usury, 92, *see also riba'* and banking

vernacular Scripture, 68
verbalism, 16, 33, 66
   problems in, 24, 26, 27
vested interests, 60, 129
   inherent in power, 58
vetoes, mutual, 72, 90
vicarious, the, 52, 90
   absent in Islam, 7, 96, 97, *see also*
   wizra
victory, 42, 43, 84
vigilance against *nifaq*, 61
vineyard parable, the, ix, 20, 32, 33, 35,
   36, 44, 110, 115
violence, 28; 'men of . . .', 45, 46, 47, 119
vision of God, the, 101, 108
vocabulary, 59, 67, 75, 77, 78, 80, 124
vocation, ours today, 89, 113
   of Muhammad, 23, 27, 28, 30
vulnerable, on being, 42, 52f

war, post-Hijrah, 41, 42, 61
warning, Qur'an as, 95f
witness, 41, 47, 63, 91
   pre- and post-Hijrah, 41
'womb of words', 70, 71
wonder, vi, xi, xiii
words, 15f, 19, 26, 65, 67, 90
   strategy in, 31, 38, 49, 73, 78
worship, of God, xi, xiii, 17, 75, 76, 126
   to Adam, ix, 93, 113
   plural, 19, 23
   of profits, 92, 126
wrath, divine, 98f
writings, sacred, 15f, 65f, 90
writ of readers, 52, 65f, 90
wrong, 30, 32, 35, 51, 58, 75, 96, *see also*
   zulm
   reach of, 33, 34

yoke, of learning, 82

Biblical and Quranic Passages

Biblical and Quranic Passages

Romans
5:2 and 14:10   106
12:1   13
12:18   127
12:21   39

1 Corinthians
15:24–26   130

Philippians
2:5–11   124
3:15   48

Hebrews
9:27   99
12:3   39
12:23   106

1 Peter
4:13 and 16   48

1 John
1:1–3   16
5:20   105

Revelation
21:5   103
22:4   105, 106, 130

Quranic Passages

Surah 2
30   ix, 3f, 9, 31, 35, 128
87   33, 116
106   83, 125
143   109, 122
148   127
161–162   104
233   97
255   9, 57, 111

Surah 3
6   78, 131
19   20

Surah 4
4.82   13, 66

Surah 5
3   20, 36
51   35
105   117, 127

Surah 6
54   107
91   120
148   36
152   97

Surah 7
32   97
172   ix, 55, 94, 110, 122

Surah 8
7–8   129
62   114

Surah 9
All   71

Surah 10
26   37
99   38

Surah 11
61   110

Surah 13
4   6
11   114
38–39   125
191   104

Surah 14
19   103, 104

Surah 16
59   129
101   145
103   23

Surah 17
21–39   90
106   73
111   77

Surah 18
6   30

Surah 21
16   3, 110
95–97   95
101–104   101

Surah 22
74   120

Surah 23
62   97
99–100   99
101–111   100
112–115   99
115   3

Surah 24
40   54
Surah 25
11–14   98
30   30

Quranic Passages

Surah 26		Surah 56 58, 63,	
198	23	68, 71	xi, 6, 111
		60	126
Surah 29			
45	76	Surah 65	
		7	97
Surah 30			
30	55, 121	Surah 68	
		4	23
Surah 35			
43	35	Surah 69	
		19–24	100
Surah 36			
45	7	Surah 70	
		41	126
Surah 37			
87	36	Surah 73	
		5	117
Surah 38			
27	104, 110	Surah 75	
		36	117
Surah 39			
22	54	Surah 76	
56–59	103	24	30
67	120		
		Surah 77	
Surah 41		1	5
41	30		
44	23	Surah 78	
		31–37	100
Surah 42			
7	22	Surah 79	
		1–14	98
Surah 44			
38	3, 110	Surah 81	
		8–9	129
Surah 48			
29	54, 121	Surah 85	
60	36	22	22
Surah 49		Surah 86	
14–17	61	1	5
		11–14	98
Surah 50			
16	104	Surah 90	
25–35	96	2	23
37	112		
		Surah 94	
Surah 51		4	23, 30
51–53	30		
		Surah 96	
Surah 53		1	66, 129
2	23		
4	73	Surah 100	
10	19	All	71
11	73		
19–23	43	Surah 101	
		1–5	98
Surah 54			
1	98	Surah 111	
		All	71
		Surah 114	
		All	51